26.95

The Best
SELF-ESTEEM
ACTIVITIES

For The Elementary Grades

Terri Akin • David Cowan • Gerry Dunne
Susanna Palomares • Dianne Schilling • Sandy Schuster

 INNERCHOICE PUBLISHING

ISBN 0-9625486-2-6

For information about Self-Esteem Workshops and other materials, please write or call:

INNERCHOICE PUBLISHING
P.O. BOX 1185
TORRANCE, CALIFORNIA 90505
Tel. (310) 816-3085   Fax (310) 816-3092

Editor: Dianne Schilling
Illustrator: Zoe Wentz

Preface

The authors are a group of experienced educators who work cooperatively to create innovative programs that reflect proven strategies of teaching and learning.

Education continues to assume more and more of the responsibility of guiding, nurturing and developing our nation's youth. This coupled with the recent explosion of interest in self esteem prompted the development of this curriculum guide of self-esteem activities.

Because we respect the demands on your time, we gave high priority to activities that can be integrated into the core curriculum. We created activities that expand the focus of teaching because we truly believe students achieve far more when thinking, feeling, physical sensing, and intuition—all major functions of the brain—are involved in the learning process.

We encourage you to integrate these activities into your classroom in ways that fit your personal style and needs.

The Authors

Table of Contents

I had a great feeling of relief when I began to understand that a youngster needs more than just subject matter. Oh, I know mathematics well, and I teach it well. I used to think that that was all I needed to do. Now I teach children, not math. I accept the fact that I can only succeed partially with some of them. I have found further that *my own personhood has educatable value.* When I don't have to know all the answers, I seem to have more answers than before when I tried to be the expert. The youngster who really made me understand this was Eddie. I asked him one day why he thought he was doing so much better than last year. He gave meaning to my whole new orientation. "It's because I like myself now when I'm with you," he said.

. . . from *Man, the Manipulator*

Self-Esteem, An Emotional Result

It is amazing how some of life's most meaningful lessons are learned. An unsought experience can create a visceral impact no textbook could possibly make. Such was the case for me one night when I was enabled to view the workings of love and self-esteem with exceptional clarity. It happened in the most unlikely place...

The first time I saw Tony we were both being "held" in a waiting area in Chicago's O'Hare Airport before boarding the same jumbo jet bound for San Diego. Looking around at the restless crowd, I saw him sitting in a wheelchair, mechanically fanning the pages of a magazine. One glance told me he was retarded.

The next time I saw Tony was aboard the plane. He was my seatmate.

Actually, Tony's mother sat in the middle seat between us, with Tony next to the window. I smiled and started to lose myself in a book. But it was impossible to ignore the drama between mother and son taking place so close at hand. Before I knew it, Tony's mother, Yvonne, and I were deeply engaged in conversation.

"You know, this trip may be a bit rough, but we're all going to make it just fine," Yvonne said as she wiped Tony's chin with kleenex. "Tony can settle down and look at pictures in magazines. Can't you, big guy?" She chuckled affectionately.

Tony wiggled and mischievously focused his eyes on hers for a split second, then mine, before letting them return to an open gaze at some point above him.

That got my attention. "How can she be so positive and loving?" I asked myself. Tentatively, I began asking questions about Tony. I learned about his age (twelve) and physical handicaps—almost total incapacitation. However, these factors were not the mainstay of the conversation. Rather, during the flight, Yvonne primarily talked about Tony and her life as his mother in a positive context. At a certain point, I realized: *this woman is bragging!*

"He's doing better all the time," she stated proudly. "For the first six years of his life he could hardly hold up his head. They told me he'd probably never improve, but gradually he learned to sit in a chair without falling out. Now he's starting to use a walker. Chances are he'll walk someday without holding on to anything. I'm so impressed with him because he's really trying. He wants to grow and develop!"

As amazed and impressed as I was with a mother who chose to attune herself to her child's achievements, regardless of their level, I was also deeply affected by the boy himself. To the best of his ability, Tony "tuned into" everything his mother said. There were clear indications that he knew he was the topic of the conversation. He was unable to add a single word, but he realized his developing abilities were being recounted. And he made efforts to reach out.

At one point he played a little joke on his mother, pretending to jump out the window. When she dramatically protested, his body jiggled with laughter. And I was laughing too, along with Tony and Yvonne. Just before we parted in San Diego, Yvonne told Tony, "Gerry has to go away now." Tears sprang into his eyes, which naturally set off a few in mine. He clasped my hand, then kissed it.

I have reflected on this experience many times. It was a brief, but enormously enriching event, in which my life became intertwined with two people who radiated love. As a result of the caring he receives on all levels from his mother, Tony is a secure, developing human being who likes and believes in himself. *He possesses an enviable amount of self-esteem!*

What is Self Esteem?

Everyone has a sense of what self-esteem is, but definitions offered by educators and psychologists vary widely. To synthesize these definitions let us say that...

...self-esteem is the emotional result of an ever-changing collection of accurate and/or inaccurate assessments one continually makes of oneself. The assessments are based on the way one _views_ oneself (self-image) and _thinks about_ oneself (self-concept) relative to numerous personal characteristics such as physical appearance, ability to learn in all realms, talents, skills, personality traits, status in various groups, and the like.

Further:

Most assessments are greatly influenced by the interaction between one's environment and one's current inner development, and are manifested in behavior. The most crucial elements in one's environment are _other people_, including caretakers, siblings, teachers, peers, and other significant persons, and the value those people place on the individual's characteristics and/or the individual as a person.

In short...

...self-esteem is the way one _feels_ about oneself—the sum _value_ one places on oneself.

Let us consider this definition in

relation to Tony. Despite his mental retardation, Tony's emotions are keen. He feels, and he knows how he feels. This was made obvious by smiles, laughter, and tears appropriate to events in his environment. Tony's self-image is undoubtedly muted, but he clearly knows he is a self, with his own ability to affect others and the general environment. This was demonstrated by his playful effort to jump out of the window. We can only guess at how much Tony understands, but it can be assumed he knows he isn't like other people who have abilities he lacks. He is surely limited in his ability to assess himself. Nonetheless Tony has feelings about himself and to a large measure they are positive.

Tony's self-esteem results more from his mother's patience, love and support than from any other influence. Her sustained presence and caring treatment produce powerful results. Interestingly enough, Yvonne did not seem to resent Tony's limitations, but instead, concentrated her attention on his "improvements" and her role as encourager.

Why is Self Esteem So Important?

A critical relationship exists between self-esteem and fulfillment of developmental potential. The central point of this true story about Tony is that because he values himself, despite his limits, he is pushing those limits. Nathaniel Branden in the book *The Psychology of Self Esteem* (1971) stated:

There is no value-judgment more important to man—no factor more decisive in his psychological development and motivation—than the estimate he passes on himself.

Compared to people of normal intelligence, the rate and degree of Tony's development is not impressive. Yet he functions more effectively as time passes. He may never walk by himself, as his mother hopes. But we can be certain he will do it if his biology permits. How many of us are as fortunate to come so close to reaching the limits of our own potential?

Self-esteem is vitally important because without it individuals cannot become what they could otherwise. For this reason, research linking self-esteem to academic, occupational and social success abounds. It is too voluminous to cite. In describing the effects of an individual's self-assessment on his daily life, Branden goes on to explain:

> *This (self) estimate is ordinarily experienced by him, not in the form of a conscious, verbalized judgment, but in the form of a feeling, a feeling that can be hard to isolate and identify because he experiences it constantly; it is part of every other feeling, it is involved in his every emotional response.*

Like a view through colored glasses, one's self-evaluation is a pervasive attitude unquestioningly experienced within oneself and displayed in virtually every life experience. Since each person is with him or herself constantly from birth to death, these cumulative feelings about self can result in a full, fruitful life or one that is unfulfilling and miserable.

How Does Self Esteem Develop?

In discussing and diagramming the hierarchical nature of human needs in his book, *Toward a Psychology of Being,* Abraham Maslow clearly articulated needs every individual must have met in order to arrive at the growth needs essential for the actualization of full potential. You probably have seen the diagram before, but let's take another look.

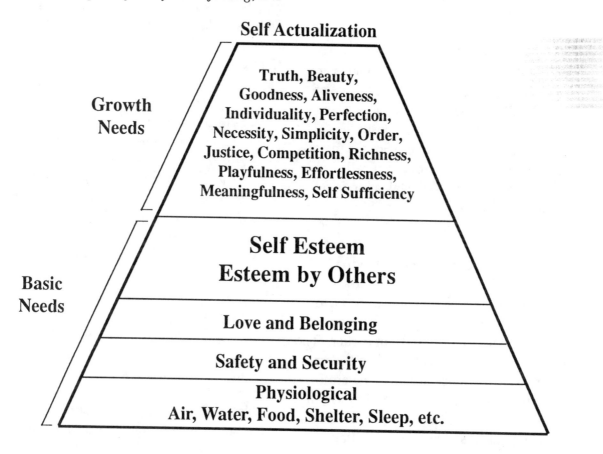

Self Actualization

Growth Needs

Truth, Beauty,
Goodness, Aliveness,
Individuality, Perfection,
Necessity, Simplicity, Order,
Justice, Competition, Richness,
Playfulness, Effortlessness,
Meaningfulness, Self Sufficiency

**Self Esteem
Esteem by Others**

Basic Needs

Love and Belonging

Safety and Security

Physiological
Air, Water, Food, Shelter, Sleep, etc.

Notice that self-esteem is the critical juncture before the self-actualization needs may be embarked upon. Now let's examine what leads to self-esteem in our quest to understand how it develops.

The diagram shows that once individuals find a favorable external environment for need satisfaction, they must have their physiological, safety, and security needs met. Next, they must belong to at least one social group where they are loved and cared for. The stage is now set for self-esteem. But note that Maslow specifically indicated esteem by others *precedes* self-esteem! This factor is rarely focused upon directly and warrants our attention.

One's self-esteem or self-dissatisfaction in large measure is simply a reflection of the ways in which one perceives oneself to be judged by significant others. Individuals are particularly prone to accept and adopt these judgments (without critically examining them) during the early years of their lives when they are most impressionable. Although one's self-evaluation is constantly in a state of flux to some degree throughout the life cycle, it is during childhood that initial self-assessments are most fluid and subject to the influence of others. Childhood is also the time when the vast array of influences most profoundly affect each person. For the majority of people, the tone for a generally positive or negative self-evaluation is set during the first two decades of life.

Evaluation of self may largely reflect the judgments of others, but it is *formed* by the self and, in turn, affects the individual who forms it. People constantly assess themselves in relation to numerous factors, creating the "ever-changing collection of self-assessments," we spoke of earlier. The emotional result of this collection becomes a pervasive influence, usually a determinant, for feelings about oneself in relation to new experiences. In other words, they constitute the axiomatic self-fulfilling prophecy. It could be said that self-esteem is like fuel we generate ourselves, which, in turn, propels us to become our optimum selves. Conversely, self-dissatisfaction is the noxious substance we create that poisons us against ourselves.

Bringing Self Esteem to the Classroom

Teachers who understand the crucial relationship between self-esteem and learning can use this book to their advantage. Increasingly, more teachers have become aware of this relationship and desire tools to assist them in their efforts with students. Presenting interesting academic experiences that challenge students yet offer them optimum chances for success is fundamentally important, but teachers can do more. They can *directly* enhance the self-esteem of their students. Additionally, many teachers are concerned that components of their own self-esteem may be lacking. Virginia Satir pointedly addressed this dilemma in her foreword to *Enhancing Self Esteem* by Frey and Carlock:

> *People are constantly prodded to have self-confidence—confidence in self, which means to value self. Hardly any of these proddings show how one can take that long journey from low self-worth to self-confidence. Coming to self-confidence, high self-worth, is a long journey, but not necessarily in time. It is more in awareness and knowledge. What does one have to experience to become aware of, to learn about, to accomplish this?*

Once formed, is one's self-evaluation "locked in?"

No! Teachers who genuinely care about their students, and themselves, can "engineer events" designed to reorder their students' self assessments, and their own, in positive directions. Most teachers motivated to do this intuitively realize how their own level of self-esteem serves as an influence on their students. Self-esteeming teachers serve students as encouraging models. Thus, these teachers consciously embark on a path to consistently accelerate their own self-esteem.

This is a challenging enterprise. Individuals cannot "will" generalized esteem for themselves, but they can *improve* their self-esteem through a disciplined course of experiences. To improve self-esteem, people must first allow themselves to learn new information about themselves and the human condition. They must consciously embark on a program to develop and practice new skills. And they must select and create environments, including people, that nurture them and foster their growth and development. Teachers can do these things for themselves and they can do them for their students!

Gerry Dunne, Ph.D.
October, 1990

Dr. Dunne is co-creator and author of the Magic Circle Program. She is a well known educator and trainer specializing in human development.

Welcome to The BEST . . .

The Theory

The theory foundation of *The BEST Self Esteem Activities for the Elementary Grades* has been developing for over twenty-five years. Originally conceived as the Human Development Program, it has been refined and expanded by Innerchoice Publishing to reflect the growing body of research in learning strategies, human relations, and organizational development. Embracing the broadest definition of "organizational," this latter area is important because we exist in a social world where our most significant learnings and experiences derive from organizational relationships. These range from our simplest contact with others to our deepest, most complex and intimate personal relationships, including that most vital relationship—the one we have with ourselves.

A Definition of Self-Esteem

Because *The BEST* is a self-esteem based collection of activities, discussion of its theory ought to be preceded by a definition and description of self-esteem. We offer the following:

Self-esteem is the sum of all that we have come to believe about ourselves in a *qualitative* sense. It is our unique perception of our worth and worthiness.

Self-esteem is fluid; that is, it is constantly subject to change. Changes in self-esteem occur in response to specific experiences—both deliberate and natural—and, in a narrower sense, simply because our perceptions of ourselves vary from environment to environment. For example, a child may esteem him/herself more at home than at school; an adult may esteem him/herself more at work than at home—or vice versa. In summary, our self-esteem is the reflection of our belief about self colored by an ever changing environmental landscape.

We have charge over our self-esteem and possess the capacity to change it. However, the *current* state of our self-esteem determines the quality of our experience in every situation. If we have done nothing to enhance our self-esteem, we are its servant, for better or worse. On the other hand, if we know how to control our self-esteem—and choose to do so—it serves as an invaluable resource *to us*.

Our self-esteem is like clay in a potter's hand. We can mold of it what we will.

Basic Assumptions of Worth and Worthiness

In order to create an environment that enhances self-esteem, activities in *The BEST* are designed to reflect these basic assumptions about human worth and worthiness:

- **There is no ceiling on self-esteem.**
- **Every individual is inherently worthwhile.**
- **Each person has the right to be self-determinlng.**
- **Everyone needs and deserves attention, acceptance and affection.**
- **Successes in life nourish the growth of self-esteem.**
- **Self-esteem is enhanced by the development and acknowledgement of identifiable skills and attributes.**

The basic purpose of *The BEST* is to create an environment in which children can become instrumental in their own growth and development.

If we believe there is **no ceiling on self-esteem**, we will be prepared to see children (and ourselves) learn, grow, and enjoy life—perhaps more than we had previously thought possible. If we believe that **every human being is worthwhile**, our interactions with children will reflect this attitude. We will not see any child as being inherently unimportant, worthless, or bad. *The BEST* reflects the belief that all human beings are valuable, and that each individual is responsible—and must answer—for his/her own behavior.

If every person has the right to **self-determination**, we have a responsibility to make opportunities for expression and actualization known to children and then facilitate their progress as they move toward the goals they choose. Self-esteem activities such as those in *The BEST* help children become aware of their own abilities and strengths and how those have been effective in overcoming obstacles they have faced in the past. In addition, it helps children develop essential skills for achieving present and future goals.

If every person has the right to receive **attention, acceptance, and affection**, we need to listen to children when they express their feelings and ideas, and help them learn to do this for each other. When genuine attention and acceptance are given and received, affection between people is free to grow. *The BEST* consistently provides a framework for realizing these ideals.

The BEST assumes that a key avenue to maintaining and enhancing self-esteem and well-being is through the process of **verbal interaction**. Our emotional and intellectual lives are so complex that we would be devastated if we could not discuss our experiences with one another. When we share our experiences and feelings at a level beyond superficiality, we see the basic commonalties among human beings and the individual differences, too.

If we believe that **successes in life nourish the growth of self-esteem**, we will give children many opportunities to experience success. Not success in a general sense, but specific successes associated with competencies.

We will help children recognize that success reflects more than just an outcome; it also applauds the process by which it was realized. Therefore, *how* we do something is as important as *what* we do.

Consider the excitement you feel when you solve a particularly difficult puzzle. Then ponder the frustration that accompanies the realization that you *don't know how you did it!* In an effort to recreate the result, you focus on the process. As each new effort fails, it is cataloged so as not to be repeated. Then it happens. You solve the puzzle again. You experience the same thrill as before, but now it is magnified by the knowledge that you possess the process for repeating it again. This is the kind of success experienced by Edison with the light bulb, by Bell with the telephone, and by every person who has recognized a need or problem, and created or discovered a solution for it. *This is the success that we must acknowledge in ourselves and others.*

If we believe that **self-esteem is enhanced by the development and acknowledgement of identifiable skills and attributes**, we will show children what those skills and attributes are, and we will give children many opportunities to practice them. In addition, we will encourage children to acknowledge themselves and one another for every increment of progress.

We frequently overlook these critical skills and attributes because they are *non-academic*. Yet all people, young and old, require them. Research demonstrates that when deficiencies in their development exist, individuals are "at risk." On the other hand, as they are developed, performance goes up and self-esteem is enhanced. This holds true for all socioeconomic levels, all cultures, and for every other environmental condition or circumstance. *The BEST* addresses these skills and attributes repeatedly through activities and discussion topics. They are:

- listening
- oral communication
- trusting
- reliability/dependability/responsibility
- understanding of others (empathy)
- adaptability
- assertiveness
- initiative/work ethic
- decision making

- time management
- goal setting
- stress management
- leadership
- problem solving

As we develop necessary skills and attributes, they are reflected in accumulated successes. These refine and sharpen the accuracy of our perception of self and the value we assign to that perception. Here is a visual model that reflects the mechanics of this relationship:

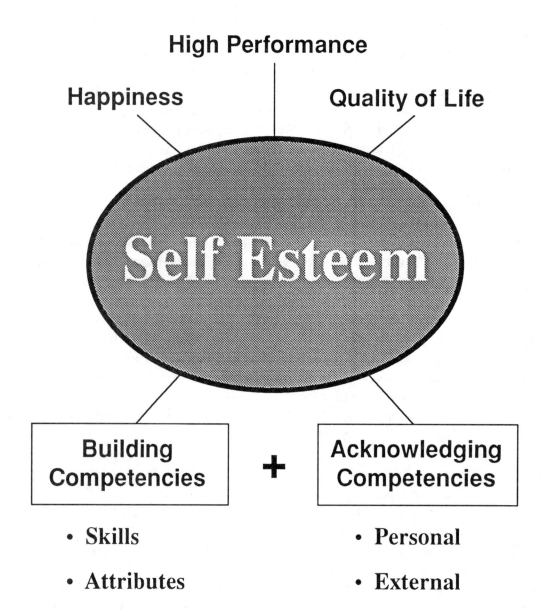

Fundamental Life Questions

As they grow and develop, children begin to ask themselves some very basic questions about life and living. One of these questions is, **"Who am I?"** The ability to answer this question at all reflects awareness of self. Many children answer the question negatively or evasively, which may reflect what they have learned about themselves from a hostile or non-supportive environment, or from a simple lack of self-awareness.

Students also ask themselves, **"What can I do?"** Their constant testing of their physical, mental, emotional, and verbal powers often drives us to fits of distraction. Positive responses to this question reflect a degree of success in accomplishing goals. Negative responses, on the other hand, are often a result of an environment that does not recognize their constructive efforts or help them to discharge their energies in positive directions.

Students, in a variety of verbal and nonverbal ways, are also trying to find out **"Can I get along with people?"** Students who answer positively tend to feel comfortable and accepted by their peers and significant others. Negative responses originate out of fears regarding their social relations and skepticism regarding their social roles.

Students who consistently answer these questions in the negative usually grow up with great difficulty. If they have the time and money, they may visit a therapist, whose diagnosis is likely to state that the client has psychological problems in one or more of the following categories: (1) a lack of awareness or avoidance of his/her own emotions, impulses, motivations, and behavior; (2) a feeling of incompetence or; (3) an inability to function adequately in a social milieu. When we consider the debilitating problems that face many human beings, *we* may well ask, "Are these kinds of difficulties inevitable in the lives of individuals? Can something be done to prevent these kinds of problems?"

A Dynamic Response

There is reason to believe it is possible to effect a positive change in the emotional and social development of human beings when they are young by intervening in their lives in such a way as to ensure awareness, social facility, and self-esteem. This kind of intervention is the purpose of the *The BEST*, which relates to three critical areas of human functioning: (1) awareness (of the feelings, thoughts, and behavior of self and others); (2) social relations (how individuals get along with other people); and (3) self-esteem (how individuals perceive their worth and worthiness). For purposes of brevity these areas are called **Awareness, Social Interaction**, and **Mastery**. They comprise the underlying theoretical components of the entire collection of activities.

Students relate to others verbally in sharing circles as each topic is discussed. They also learn to listen. The activities provide practice in basic communication skills, while subject matter relating to relevant life issues is being discussed. This provides positive experiences which offer children the opportunity to grow in awareness, to learn more about effective modes of social interaction, and to feel more masterful (self-confident).

The BEST serves as a way of developing, maintaining, and enhancing life skills. The experiences gained from participating in sharing circles can contribute to the reservoir of strength from which we may draw when difficult life circumstances occur.

The following are descriptions of the three growth areas of the activities.

Awareness

Awareness is a critical element of self-esteem. Aware people do not hide things from themselves. They are in touch with the inner world of their feelings and thoughts, and they are in control of their actions—and they understand that other people feel, think, and behave too. They are also in touch with the reality of the past, the possibilities of the future, and the certainty of the present. Awareness allows individuals to order their lives flexibly and effectively on a moment-to-moment basis.

By contrast, unawareness of what is going on in one's inner and/or outer worlds sets the stage for lack of congruence between what one believes or feels and how one behaves. Feelings of isolation ("I'm the only one who's ever felt like this before.") occur when people are unaware that everyone experiences the same triad of human functioning (feeling, thinking, and behaving) that they do. Unaware people are not in charge of their own lives. By default, their courses are plotted by others or by parts of themselves they have not recognized.

We hope to demonstrate experientially to children, through their involvement with the *The BEST* activities, that everyone experiences all the emotions. Sharing circle topics, supporting activities, and experience sheets provide opportunities for children to experience and discuss their emotions in an accepting and nonthreatening atmosphere. Students discover that emotions cannot be judged right or wrong, good or bad, in a moral sense. They simply are. To try to negate one's feelings or attempt to take away a feeling in someone else only compounds the situation—as neuroses, insomnia, ulcers, and miscommunication between persons testifies. For this reason the feelings of each child are focused on and accepted in every sharing circle. As Carl Rogers states in *On Becoming a Person*::

...when I can accept another person, which means specifically accepting the feelings and attitudes and beliefs that he has as a real and vital part of him, then I am assisting him to become a person, and there seems to me great value in this.

Similar to a feeling, a thought, in and of itself, can hurt no one. The cognition phase of the sharing circle enables children to share their thoughts in a constructive manner. They become aware that even divergent thoughts may be discussed without fear. Students realize that their ability to think is a great power, and may be used constructively or destructively in a multitude of ways. Through their participation in the activities, children become more aware of how often they personally use their thought processes to make life meaningful and productive.

Social Interaction

People effective in their social interactions are capable of understanding other people. They know how to interact with others flexibly, skillfully, and responsibly, without sacrificing their own needs and integrity. They have a good sense of timing and are effective at being heard and making needed changes in their environment. These people can process nonverbal as well as verbal messages of others, and they realize that people have the power to affect one another. They are aware, not only of how others affect them, but also of the effect of their behavior on others, and they take accompanying responsibility for their actions.

Without skills in social interaction, individuals confuse situations and give inappropriate responses. They lack positive communication skills and are unaware of how their actions affect others.

According to Harvey Jackins, author of *The Human Side of Human Beings*, every person is inherently intelligent, zestful, and capable of loving, cooperative relationships with others. What goes wrong is that we get hurt, and repeated hurts significantly affect those same inherent gifts. We then have great difficulty liking, trusting, and sometimes even respecting others, and they have the same difficulties with us. Our social interactions suffer, and we do not enjoy each other as we potentially could.

Logically, the next question is, "What can we do about this situation?" Students deal with other people every day—their peers and significant adults. They need positive interpersonal experiences and information in the social realm in order to offset prior difficulties and build healthy relationships. Yet, as Carl Rogers points out, the educational system has largely failed to in any systematic way meet the need of children to learn how to understand and get along with other people.

If they are fortunate, children are surrounded by people who give them attention. In the case of people older than they, it is highly desirable that healthy, responsible behavior be modeled. If children are listened to, if their feelings are accepted, and if they learn how to do this with others, they are indeed fortunate.

The BEST activities attempt to actualize the positive qualities that are inherent in all of us. By their format and process, they allow children to practice positive modes of communication and transfer them to other situations.

The BEST gives children opportunities to discuss what goes into a relationship that makes it friendly, caring, and trusting. Further, children explore problem areas in varied human settings. Society has an ideal view of how people should ultimately behave, but no formal structure that defines or describes the intermediate steps. *The BEST* helps to develop and nurture an understanding of those intermediate steps.

Mastery

Self-confident people believe in themselves; they perceive themselves as being "okay." They are not debilitated by knowledge of their weaknesses, but have a healthy degree of self-esteem and a feeling of mastery or self-confidence. They try new challenges and do not strongly fear failure. It is likely that they have experienced success more than failure, and probably when they were successful, a significant person noted it and commented on it to them.

It has been widely observed that individuals are likely to achieve mastery in their endeavors when they have a feeling of mastery about themselves. Generally, it seems as though people who believe in themselves are the ones who continue to succeed, and the more they succeed, the more they believe in themselves. Thus, a beneficial cycle is created.

The ways in which significant others respond to what we do plays a critical role in whether or not we see ourselves as masterful. If they let us know they recognize our efforts and comment positively when we try or succeed, our awareness that we do have capabilities increases. Conversely, without favorable comment we are less aware of our capabilities, even if we experience success. This explains why so many brilliant people do not regard themselves as such. Rather, they are painfully aware of their limitations and shortcomings and miss many opportunities to actualize their potential. Our culture has numerous ways of causing us to focus on our weaknesses rather than our assets and abilities.

In *The BEST*, we call belief in oneself a feeling of "I can-ness." Through the sharing circles, supporting activities, and experience sheets, children are routinely encouraged to explore their own successes and hear positive comments about their efforts. All the activities are designed to heighten students' awareness of their own and others' successes. Failure is a reality that is also examined. The objective, however, is not to remind children that they have failed; instead these activities enable them to see that falling short is a common, universal experience.

History speaks to us of many effective and capable individuals who found great success in their endeavors. Some, however, achieved success for themselves at the expense of others. They exercised their abilities and powers irresponsibly. By focusing on their positive behaviors and accomplishments, children recognize the rewards that can be gained when one behaves responsibly. Cooperation vs. competition is another issue addressed by the mastery portion of the activities. As equitably as possible, the activities attempt to meet the needs of all children in the group. Everyone's feelings are accepted. Comparisons and judgments are not made. The circle is not another competitive arena, but is guided by a spirit of cooperation. When children practice fair, respectful, noncompetitive interaction with each other, they benefit from the experience and are likely to employ these responsible behaviors in other life situations. The fringe lesson is: there need be no losers in order to have winners in a group.

The BEST has been developed to help children deal with such matters as improving their learning habits, taking pride in their accomplishments, dealing rationally with disappointments and problems, and making workable decisions. It is not the aim of *The BEST* to participate in producing a masterful but limited child. Rather, we hope to help children become responsibly competent.

Organizing Sharing Circles

Group Size and Composition

Sharing circles are a time for focusing on individuals' contributions in an unhurried fashion. For this reason, each sharing circle group needs to be kept relatively small—eight to twelve usually works best at the middle to upper elementary grades. At this age, children are capable of extensive verbalization. You will want to encourage this, and not stifle them because of time constraints. For the younger children, smaller circles might work best.

Each group should be as **heterogeneous** as possible with respect to sex, ability, and racial/ethnic background. Sometimes there will be a group in which all the children are particularly reticent to speak. At these times, bring in an expressive child or two who will get things going. Sometimes it is necessary for practical reasons to change the membership of a group. Once established, however, it is advisable to keep a group as stable as possible.

Length and Location of Sharing Circles

Most sharing circles last approximately 20 to 30 minutes, sometimes a little longer. At first children tend to be reluctant to express themselves fully because they do not yet know that the circle is a safe place. Consequently your first sessions may not last more than 10 to 15 minutes. Generally speaking, children become comfortable and motivated to speak with continued experience.

Sharing circles may be conducted at any time during the day and may be carried out wherever there is room for children to sit in a circle and experience few or no distractions. Most leaders prefer to have children sit in chairs rather than on the floor. Students seem to be less apt to invade one another's space while seated in chairs. Some leaders conduct sessions outdoors, with children seated in a secluded, grassy area.

How to Get Started

Teachers and counselors have used numerous methods to involve children in the circle process. What works well for one leader or class does not always work for another. Here are two basic strategies leaders have successfully used to set up groups. Whichever you use, we recommend that you post a chart listing the sharing circle rules and procedures to which every participant may refer (see "Leading Sharing Circles").

1. Start one group at a time, and cycle through all groups. If possible, provide an opportunity for every child to experience a sharing circle in a setting where there are no disturbances. This may mean arranging for another staff member or aide to take charge of the children not participating in the circle. Non-participants may work on course work or experience sheets, or, if you have a cooperative librarian, they may be sent to the library to work independently or in small groups on a class assignment. Repeat this procedure until all of the children have been involved in at least one sharing circle.

Next, initiate a class discussion about the sharing circles. Explain that from now on you will be meeting with each circle group in the classroom, with the remainder of the class present. Ask the children to help you plan established procedures for the remainder of the class to follow.

Meet with each sharing circle group on a different day, systematically cycling through the groups. In your second or third cycle, begin student leadership training. In

each group, allow a student the opportunity to lead the session as you sit beside him/her, acting as leader-trainer. In time, student-led groups may meet independently at staggered times during the period, or they may meet simultaneously in different parts of the room while you circulate. Eventually you should be able to be a participant in the student-led groups. For more information on student leadership, refer to the heading, "Training Student Leaders" later in this section.

2. Combine inner and outer circles. Meet with one sharing circle group while another group listens and observes as an outer circle. Then have the two groups change places, with the children on the outside becoming the inner circle, and responding verbally to the topic. Later, a third group may be added to this alternating cycle. The end product of this arrangement is two or more groups (comprising everyone in the class) meeting together simultaneously. While one group is involved in discussion, the other groups listen and observe as members of an outer circle. *Invite the members of the outer circle to participate in the review and discussion phases of the circle.*

What to Do with the Rest of the Class

A number of arrangements can be made for children who are not participating in sharing circles. Here are some ideas:

- **Arrange the room to ensure privacy.** This may involve placing a circle of chairs or carpeting in a corner, away from other work areas. You might construct dividers from existing furniture, such as bookshelves or screens, or simply arrange chairs and tables in such a way that the circle area is protected from distractions.
- **Involve aides, counselors, parents, or fellow teachers.** Have an aide conduct a lesson with the rest of the class while

you meet with a circle group. If you do not have an aide assigned to you, use auxiliary staff or volunteer parents.

- **Have students work quietly on subject-area assignments in pairs or small, task-oriented groups.**
- **Utilize student aides or leaders.** If the seat-work activity is in a content area, appoint children who show ability in that area as "consultants," and have them assist other children.
- **Give the students plenty to do.** List assignments on the board. Make materials for quiet individual activities available so that children cannot run out of things to do and be tempted to consult you or disturb others.
- **Make the activity of students outside the circle enjoyable.** When you can involve the rest of the class in something meaningful to them, they will probably be less likely to interrupt the circle.
- **Have the students work on an ongoing project.** When they have a task in progress, children can simply resume where they left off, with little or no introduction from you. In these cases, appointing a "person in charge," "group leader", or "consultant" is wise.
- **Allow individual journal-writing.** While a circle is in progress, have the other children make entries in a private (or share-with-teacher-only) journal. Do not correct the journals, but if you read them, be sure to respond to the entries with your own written thoughts, where appropriate.

Training Student Leaders

A basic assumption of *The BEST* is that every human being (barring those having considerable subnormal intelligence) has leadership potential. Further, the best time for energizing this ability is in childhood. Students in

countless elementary and secondary classrooms effectively lead their own sharing circles.

You can begin training student leaders after two or three successful sharing circles. Invite the children to consider volunteering to lead a circle. Suggest that they watch you closely to see what steps the leader follows. At the end of the session, ask the children to describe what you did. They should be able to delineate the following steps:

The leader:
1. announces the topic and clarifies what it is about.
2. may lead a review of the ground rules.
3. gives each person a turn who wants one.
4. may conduct a review of what each person said.
5. conducts a summary discussion by focusing on the meaning of the session and the major observations of the participants.
6. terminates the circle.

Ask the children if anyone would like to volunteer to lead the next session. If no one volunteers, accept this outcome and wait a session or two before trying again. If several volunteer, choose a student who you think is very likely to succeed. Then tell the group the topic you have in mind for the next session.

Before the next session, give the student leader a copy of the activity, and discuss it with him/her. Also provide a copy of the sharing circle rules and procedures (see "**Leading Sharing Circles**"). As the session begins, tell the group that you will be the trainer and speak about the process when necessary, but that otherwise, the student is the leader and you are a participant. Before turning the session over to the student leader add one more thing—a new ground rule stating that the children are expected to respect fully the leadership position of the student. **If they disagree with the student leader's procedure or are aware of what s/he should do next when the student leader may have forgotten, they are not to say anything at that time unless they are asked to by the student leader.** When people are learning a new skill, it can be very upsetting to have other people constantly reminding them of what they are supposed to do next. For this reason the student leader should not be heckled in any way. (Time can be taken at the end of the session for the group to give feedback to the student leader about his/her performance).

Now, allow the student leader to proceed, interjecting statements yourself about the procedure only when absolutely necessary. Be sure to take your turn and model respectful listening. As necessary, deal with children who interrupt or distract the group.

Before ending the session, thank the student leader, and conduct a brief feedback session by asking the children, "Who would like to tell (the student leader) what you liked about the way s/he conducted the session?" Let the student leader call on each person who has a comment.

Tell the children the topic you have in mind for the next session, and ask for a volunteer to lead it. Remember that students should not lead the group until you are sure they will be successful. Be careful to appoint leaders of both sexes and all racial/ethnic groups. Continue this process until all who wish to conduct circles are competent enough to lead them independently.

Combining Teacher and Student Leadership

This procedure allows several groups to meet simultaneously during the same class period.

Begin by announcing to the class that circles will be held during the day. If necessary, review the ground rules with the whole class. Then announce the topic, describe it and restate it. Finally, take your turn to relate to it personally. Answer any questions the children have, and then ask them to get into their groups.

When the circles are formed, the student leaders take over. They restate the topic and facilitate the sharing phase and, if desired, a review. The children return to their regular seating for the summary discussion, which is led by the teacher.

Note: This is a particularly fruitful procedure if you are using *The BEST* as a supplement to your regular curriculum. The summary discussion can then include questions concerning the relevancy of the topic to subject matter currently being studied.

Leading Sharing Circles

This section is a thorough guide for conducting sharing circles. It covers major points to keep in mind and answers questions which will arise as you begin using the activities. Please remember that these guidelines are presented to assist you, not to restrict you. Follow them and trust your own leadership style at the same time.

Sharing Circle Procedures

1. Setting up the circle (1-2 minutes)
2. Reviewing the ground rules (1-2 minutes) *
3. Introducing the topic (1-2 minutes)
4. Sharing by circle members (12-18 minutes)
5. Reviewing what is shared (3-5 minutes) *
6. Summary discussion (2-8 minutes)
7. Closing the circle (less than 1 minute)
   *optional

Setting up the circle (1-2 minutes)

As you sit down with the children in the circle, remember that you are not teaching a lesson. You are facilitating a group of people. Establish a positive atmosphere. In a relaxed manner, address each child by name, using eye contact and conveying warmth. An attitude of seriousness blended with enthusiasm will let the children know that the sharing circle is an important learning experience—an activity that can be interesting and meaningful.

Reviewing the ground rules (1-2 minutes).

At the beginning of the first session, and at appropriate intervals thereafter, go over the ground rules for the sharing circle. They are:

Sharing Circle Rules

1. Bring yourself to the circle and nothing else.
2. Everyone gets a turn to share, including the leader.
3. You can skip your turn if you wish.
4. Listen to the person who is sharing.
5. The time is shared equally.
6. Stay in your own space.
7. There are no interruptions, probing, put-downs, or gossip.

From this point on, demonstrate to the children that you expect them to remember and abide by the ground rules. Convey that you think well of them and know they are fully capable of responsible behavior. Let them know that by coming to the session they are making a commitment to listen and show acceptance and respect for the other children and you.

Introducing the topic (1-2 minutes)

State the topic in your own words. Elaborate and provide examples as each activity suggests. Add clarifying statements of your own that will help the children understand the topic. Answer questions about the topic, and emphasize that there are no "right" responses. Finally, restate the topic, opening the session to responses (theirs and yours). Sometimes taking your turn first helps the children understand the aim of the topic. At various points throughout the session, state the topic again.

Just prior to leading a sharing circle, contemplate the topic and think of at least one possible response that *you* can make to it.

Sharing by circle members (12-18 minutes)

The most important point to remember is this: The purpose of the sharing circle is to give children an opportunity to express themselves and be accepted for the experiences, thoughts, and feelings they share. Avoid taking the action away from the circle members. They are the stars!

Reviewing what is shared (optional 3-5 minutes)

Besides modeling effective listening (the very best way to teach it) and positively reinforcing children for attentive listening, a review can be used to deliberately improve listening skills in circle members.

Reviewing is a time for reflective listening, when circle members feed back what they heard each other say during the sharing phase of the circle. Besides encouraging effective listening, reviewing provides circle members with additional recognition. It validates their experience and conveys the idea, "you are important," a message we can all profit from hearing often.

To review, a circle member simply addresses someone who shared, and briefly paraphrases what the person said ("John, I heard you say....").

The first few times you conduct reviews, stress the importance of checking with the speaker to see if the review accurately summarized the main things that were shared. If the speaker says, "No," allow him/her to make corrections. Stress too, the importance of speaking *directly* to the speaker, using the person's name and the pronoun "you," not "he" or "she." If someone says, "S/he said that...," intervene as promptly and respectfully as possible and say to the reviewer, "Talk to Betty...Say you." This is very important. The person whose turn is being reviewed will have a totally different feeling when talked *to*, instead of *about*.

Note: Remember that the review is optional and is most effective when used *occasionally*, not as a part of every circle.

Summary discussion (2-8 minutes)

The summary discussion is the cognitive portion of the sharing circle. During this phase, the leader asks thought-provoking questions to stimulate free discussion and higher-level thinking. Each sharing circle in the book includes three or more summary questions; however, at times you may want to formulate questions that are more appropriate to the level of understanding in your group—or to what was actually shared in the circle. If you wish to make connections between the sharing circle topic and a particular subject area, ask questions that will accomplish that objective and allow the summary discussion to extend longer.

It is important that you not confuse the summary with the review. The review is optional; the summary is not. The summary meets the need of people of all ages to find meaning in what they do. Thus, the summary serves as a necessary culmination to each sharing circle by allowing the children to clarify the key concepts they gained from the session.

Closing the circle (less than 1 minute).

The ideal time to end a sharing circle is when the summary discussion reaches natural closure. Sincerely thank everyone for being part of the circle. Don't thank specific students for speaking, as doing so might convey the impression that speaking is more appreciated than mere listening. Then close the circle by saying, "The sharing circle is over," or "Okay, that ends our session."

More about Sharing Circle Procedures and Rules

The next few paragraphs offer further clarification concerning sharing circle leadership.

Why should students bring themselves to the circle and nothing else? Individual teachers differ on this point, but most prefer that children not bring objects (such as pencils, books, etc.) to the circle that may be distracting.

Who gets to talk? Everyone. The importance of acceptance cannot be overly stressed. In one way or another practically every ground rule says one thing: *accept one another*. When you model acceptance of students, they will learn how to be accepting. Each individual in the circle is important and deserves a turn to speak if s/he wishes to take it. Equal opportunity to become involved should be given to everyone in the circle.

Circle members should be reinforced equally for their contributions. There are many reasons why a leader may become more enthused over what one child shares than another. The response may be more on target, reflect more depth, be more entertaining, be philosophically more in keeping with one's own point of view, and so on. However, children need to be given equal recognition for their contributions, even if the contribution is to listen silently throughout the session.

In most of the sharing circles, plan to take a turn and address the topic, too. Students usually appreciate it very much and learn a great deal when their teachers and counselors are willing to tell about their own experiences, thoughts, and feelings. In this way you let your students know that you acknowledge your own humanness.

Does everyone have to take a turn? No. Students may choose to skip their turns. If the circle becomes a pressure situation in which the members are coerced in any way to speak, it will become an unsafe place where participants are not comfortable. Meaningful discussion is unlikely in such an atmosphere. By allowing students to make this choice, you are showing them that you accept their right to remain silent if that is what they choose to do.

As you begin circles, it will be to your advantage if one or more children decline to speak. If you are unperturbed and accepting when this happens, you let them know you are offering them an opportunity to experience something you think is valuable, or at least worth a try, and not attempting to force-feed them. You as a leader should not feel compelled to share a personal experience in every session, either. However, if you decline to speak in most of the sessions, this may have an inhibiting effect on the childs' willingness to share.

A word should also be said about how this ground rule has sometimes been carried to extremes. Sometimes leaders have bent over backwards to let children know they don't have to take a turn. This

seeming lack of enthusiasm on the part of the leader has caused reticence in the children. In order to avoid this outcome, don't project any personal insecurity as you lead the session. Be confident in your proven ability to work with children. Expect something to happen and it will.

Some circle leaders ask the participants to raise their hands when they wish to speak, while others simply allow free verbal sharing without soliciting the leader's permission first. Choose the procedure that works best for you, but do not call on anyone unless you can see signs of readiness.

Some leaders have reported that their first circles fell flat—that no one, or just one or two children, had anything to say. But they continued to have circles, and at a certain point everything changed. Thereafter, the children had a great deal to say that these leaders considered worth waiting for. It appears that in these cases the leaders' acceptance of the right to skip turns was a key factor. In time most children will contribute verbally when they have something they want to say, and when they are assured there is no pressure to do so.

Sometimes a silence occurs during a sharing circle. Don't feel you have to jump in every time someone stops talking. During silences children have an opportunity to think about what they would like to share or to contemplate an important idea they've heard. A general rule of thumb is to allow silence to the point that you observe group discomfort. At that point move on. *Do not switch to another topic.* To do so implies you will not be satisfied until the children speak. If you change to another topic, you are telling them you didn't really mean it when you said they didn't have to take a turn if they didn't want to.

If you are bothered about children who attend a number of circles and still do not share verbally, reevaluate what you consider to be involvement. Participation does not necessarily mean talking. Students who do not speak *are* listening and learning.

How can I encourage effective listening? The sharing circle is a time (and place) for students and leaders to strengthen the habit of listening by doing it over and over again. No one was born knowing how to listen effectively to others. It is a skill like any other that gets better as it is practiced. In the immediacy of the sharing circle, the members become keenly aware of the necessity to listen, and most children respond by expecting it of one another.

In *The BEST*, listening is defined as the respectful focusing of attention on individual speakers. It includes eye contact with the speaker and open body posture. It eschews interruptions of any kind. When you conduct a sharing circle, listen and encourage listening in the children by (1) focusing your attention on the person who is speaking, (2) being receptive to what the speaker is saying (not mentally planning your next remark), and (3) recognizing the speaker when s/he finishes speaking, either verbally ("Thanks, Shirley") or nonverbally (a nod and a smile).

To encourage effective listening in the children, reinforce them by letting them know you have noticed they were listening to each other and you appreciate it. Occasionally conducting a review after the sharing phase also has the effect of sharpening listening skills.

How can I ensure the students get equal time? When circle members share the time equally, they demonstrate their acceptance of the notion that everyone's contribution is of equal importance. It is not uncommon to have at least one dominator in a group. This person is usually totally unaware that by continuing to talk s/he is taking time from others who are less assertive.

Be very clear with the children about the purpose of this ground rule. Tell them at the outset how much time there is and whether or not you plan to conduct a review. When it is your turn, always limit your own contribution. If someone goes on and on, do intervene (dominators need to know what they are doing), but do so as gently and respectfully as you can.

What are some examples of put-downs? Put-downs convey the message, "You are not okay as you are." Some put-downs are deliberate, but many are made unknowingly. Both kinds are undesirable in a sharing circle because they destroy the atmosphere of acceptance and disrupt the flow of discussion. Typical put-downs include:
- overquestioning.
- statements that have the effect of teaching or preaching
- advice giving
- one-upsmanship
- criticism, disapproval, or objections
- sarcasm
- statements or questions of disbelief

How can I deal with put-downs? There are two major ways for dealing with put-downs in sharing circles: preventing them from occurring and intervening when they do.

Going over the ground rules with the children at the beginning of each session, particularly in the earliest sessions, is a helpful preventive technique. Another is to reinforce the children when they adhere to the rule. Be sure to use nonpatronizing, nonevaluative language.

Unacceptable behavior should be stopped the moment it is recognized by the leader. When you become aware that a put-down is occurring, do whatever you ordinarily do to stop destructive behavior in the classroom. If one child gives another an unasked-for bit of advice, say for example, "Jane, please give Alicia a chance to tell her story." To a child who interrupts say, "Ed, it's Sally's turn." In most cases the fewer words, the better—children automatically tune out messages delivered as lectures.

Sometimes children disrupt the group by starting a private conversation with the person next to them. Touch the offender on the arm or shoulder while continuing to give eye contact to the child who is speaking. If you can't reach the offender, simply remind him/her of the rule about listening. If children persist in putting others down during sharing circles, ask to see them at another time and hold a brief one-to-one conference, urging them to follow the rules. Suggest that they reconsider their membership in the circle. Make it clear that if they don't intend to honor the ground rules, they are not to come to the circle.

How can I keep students from gossiping? Periodically remind students that using names and sharing embarrassing information is not acceptable. Urge the children to relate personally to one another, but not to tell intimate details of their lives.

What should the leader do during the summary discussion? Conduct the summary as an open forum, giving students the opportunity to discuss a variety of ideas and accept those that make sense to them. Don't impose your opinions on the children, or allow the children to impose theirs on one another. Ask open-ended questions, encourage higher-level thinking, contribute your own ideas when appropriate, and act as a facilitator.

Strategies for Using *The BEST* Activities

The BEST utilizes a wide variety of techniques. The sharing circle is the central strategy, but there are others. This section describes several major strategies and presents basic points to keep in mind as you implement them.

Dyads

When first initiated, dyads are probably most effective if the children are allowed to select their own partners. After the class is well into the year and the children know each other better, ask the children to pair up with someone they've never worked with before. If the children tend to shun the opposite sex, announce that you would like to see boys and girls pair up.

Ask the children to sit close to and facing their partner, and position themselves as far away from other children as possible so they will be able to hear each other. If the number of children is uneven, be the partner of the remaining child. In fact, it is helpful for the leader to be in as many dyads as possible.

In most dyad activities, partners take turns speaking and listening in response to one or more topics. Two advantages of dyads are that they allow maximum self-expression in a relatively short time period. And they are the most effective way for children to discuss some topics.

Triads

Some triad activities are simply very small discussion groups. Others are like dyads in that the children take turns speaking and listening in response to specific topics. The difference is that the third person in the triad acts as an observer while the other two interact. The observer role is played by each member in the triad on a rotating basis. The function of the observer is to note, as objectively as possible, the behavior of the interacting pair and give them feedback.

Small Group Discussions

When children meet in small groups to discuss a topic or engage in some phase of an activity, they are usually directed to select a leader or recorder. They are also urged to observe sharing circle ground rules. The intent is not to transform every small-group task into a sharing circle, merely to provide structure and safety. One of the main advantages of small groups is that they give the children an opportunity to collaborate—which facilitates problem-solving, stimulates creativity, and takes some of the load off you.

Class Discussions

Almost all *The BEST* activities include a culminating discussion, and some activities are almost entirely discussion. When leading a discussion, act as a facilitator, keeping these guidelines in mind:
- Questions should be relevant, timely, and open-ended.
- It should be understood that there are no right or wrong answers.
- Keep the discussion focused.

Without being rigid, ask children who introduce peripheral issues to bring them up again when the main discussion is over or at some other time. Digressions can ruin the effectiveness of a discussion, but very often the other thoughts that children introduce are worth discussing, too.

Brainstorming

Brainstorming is a very valuable way to promote individual creativity and group cohesiveness simultaneously. Perhaps the most important thing to remember about brainstorming is that the generation of ideas and the evaluation of ideas are two separate processes. Thanks to this distinction, individuals may contribute their ideas spontaneously without fear of criticism. Brainstorming includes the following basic steps:
- The task or problem is defined.
- The students describe all the ideas they can think of, without evaluating any of them.

- The ideas are recorded.
- The brainstorming is ended.
- Then and only then, the ideas are evaluated.
- A choice or decision is made.

Dramatizations and Role-Playing

Besides being very dynamic, acting experiences in the classroom promote direct, experiential learning. Dramatizations usually involve planning, rehearsing, and performing, and typically call for a student director. Role-playing is more spontaneous, and unfolds in a situation that simulates reality. Although the participants are playing the parts of other people, they usually end up playing themselves, as their own values surface.

Role-playing is frequently used as a problem-solving technique in which alternative actions are tested and evaluated. Opportunities for role-playing (other then those described in the activities) may evolve from unfinished stories, films, pictures, and real or imaginary situations suggested by you and the children.

Creative Writing

Sometimes children are asked to write a story, poem, play, lyrics for a song, or even create a cartoon. Frequently the class brainstorms ideas before the writing period begins in order to motivate children and give them ideas. One way teachers have successfully encouraged children to write is by following this (or a variation of this) procedure:

The children imagine how they would *say* what they want to write, and then write down those words without regard for neatness, grammar, punctuation, spelling, etc. After they record some thoughts, they go back and read what they have written. Then they proceed with the next collection of thoughts in the same way. They continue doing this (often each collection of thoughts becomes a separate paragraph) until they have finished. At this point they go back over what they have written, reading it carefully and editing their work for grammar, syntax, spelling, and punctuation. (You may prefer to have children meet in dyads or small groups and edit each other's writing, as well as make suggestions pertaining to content and style.) As a final step, the entire product is rewritten to include all editorial changes.

If you have computers, encourage the children to use word processing, spell checkers, and any other available technology.

Research

Some activities entail various kinds of research. Students may use the school or public library or other resources. Here are some suggestions to consider when research is called for:

- Select a topic area of general interest to your students.
- Allow them to select specific topics.
- Describe where the needed information may be found.
- Be specific about your expectations with respect to their written report.

Voluminous written work should not be the object of research activities. Students are far more likely to find this kind of activity meaningful when writing is included as a means to an end, rather than an end in itself.

Art and Music

The major objective of art activities is to allow children to express their feelings and ideas creatively. You don't have to be an art teacher to involve children in activities that involve artistic expression. For example, cartooning may be an acceptable substitute for story-writing if you teach English language arts. Other examples include encouraging children to make posters, displays, timelines, charts, and other illustrations to aid them in presenting individual and group reports to the class.

Make music appreciation activities meaningful by giving the children background information on each musical selection before playing it. If the recording has been contributed by a student, ask him/her to introduce it. Before selections are played, urge the children to get into a relaxed position in their chairs. Suggest that they close their eyes. Be sure to use the best sound equipment available.

EXPRESSING FEELINGS

The ability to identify, accept and appropriately express one's feelings is a hallmark of mental/emotional health. The activities in this segment assist students to understand the universality and function of feelings and manage them effectively.

Color My Feelings

Discussion and Art

Relates to: Art and Language Arts (oral and written language)

Objective(s):   The students will:
— identify feeling words.
— select three colors to express each feeling word.
— creatively interpret feeling words through painting/drawing.

Time: approximately 40 minutes

Materials needed: chalkboard or butcher paper, chalk or magic marker, white construction paper, crayons or paints

Directions: **Ask the students to name all the words they can think of that describe feelings.** Write them on the board or butcher paper. Make sure that you have at least one word per child. If need be, add to the list yourself. Don't forget words like *surprised, confused, delighted, annoyed, frustrated, joyful, ecstatic, depressed*, etc. Discuss several possible situations that can cause each feeling.

As a class, have the students assign three colors to each feeling word. Take a vote to get a majority opinion. For example, blue, gray, and green may be selected for the word *sad;* yellow, pink, and orange may represent *joyful*. Write the three chosen color words next to each feeling word on the board or butcher paper. Don't duplicate any color combination.

Tell the students to choose one of the feeling words to illustrate.

Distribute construction paper and crayons or paints. Have the students make pictures or create designs that express the feeling words they chose. Tell them to use only the three colors that the group decided should represent that feeling. Allow plenty of time for thinking and creating, but reserve time for clean-up.

Facilitate discussion while the students work. Talk about the different feelings and the kinds of experiences that might cause each one.

Expressing the Mood

Creative Movement

Relates to:	Music and Physical Education
Objective(s):	The students will: —identify feelings generated by different styles of music. —interpret their feelings in movement.
Time:	approximately 20 minutes
Materials needed:	Tape recorder or record player; casettes or records that elicit various feelings (checked out of a local library or brought in by students). Here are some suggestions: • **Happy:** Bobby McFerrin, "Don't Worry, Be Happy;" Tchaikovsky, "Nutcracker Suite" • **Sad:** Debbie Gibson, "Silence Speaks a Thousand Words;" Tchaikovsky, "Symphony Pathetique" • **Angry:** Any heavy metal selection; Grieg, "March of the Mountain King" • **Playful:** Surfaris, "Wipeout;" Saint-Saens, "Carnival Overture" • **Scared:** Theme from "Beetlejuice;" Gustav Holst, "Mercury" • **Confident:** Theme from "Star Wars;" Madonna, "Over and Over"
Directions:	**Clear a space in a large room or go outdoors where the students can move freely.** **Play 3 to 4 minutes of each piece of music.** Have the students listen to and interpret the mood of the music by moving their bodies rhythmically. Since the students may feel self-conscious about moving, be sure to move yourself. Use your head, arms, legs, and torso. Move in upright, squatting, and reclining positions. **Lead a discussion after each selection.** Talk about the mood of the music and the feelings the students experienced while listening and moving.

Giving Form to Feelings
Living Sculptures

Relates to:	Drama and Language Arts (writing and oral language)
Objective(s):	The students will: —identify recently-experienced feelings. —demonstrate how feelings can be expressed nonverbally. —identify feelings based on body language and facial expression.
Time:	approximately 30 minutes
Materials needed:	a small sheet of paper and pencil for each student
Directions:	**Ask the students to think of 4 feelings that they've experienced today, and to write them down in the form of** *feeling words* **on their sheets of paper.** When they are through writing, have them fold the papers over to hide the writing. **As the students to choose partners.** Explain that each pair is to pick one person in the pair to be Person **A**. The other will be Person **B**. Give the students a moment to accomplish this. Then tell Person **A** to whisper one of his/her feeling words into Person **B**'s ear. Have all the pairs do this at once. Explain that Person **B**'s job is now to "sculpt" Person **A** to look as if s/he is experiencing that feeling. Demonstrate by sculpting one of the students to look worried (or some other feeling). Don't *tell* the students the feeling you are trying to capture. *Show* them: Put the student's hands together and direct him/her to "wring" them. Gently push the student's eyebrows up in the center to form worry lines. Round the student's shoulders and cause them to shake just a bit. Ask the class to guess what feeling your "sculpture" depicts. After Person **B** has finished sculpting Person **A**, have each pair join another pair to form groups of four. Tell them to guess what feeling each other's sculpture represents.

Tell the partners to switch roles. Person **B** now whispers a feeling word to Person **A** and the activity is repeated. Continue switching roles after each round until all eight feelings (four per partner) have been sculpted.

Lead a discussion. Ask several open-ended questions to help the students summarize what they have learned from the experience:

— *When you were the <u>sculptor</u>, how did you decide what to do?*

— *When you were the <u>sculpture</u>, did your partner succeed in making you look like you were feeling?*

— *What did you learn from this activity?*

A Time I Felt Happy

A Sharing Circle

Note:	Before introducing sharing circles to your students, please read "Leading Sharing Circles" beginning on page 15.

Relates to: Language Arts (oral language)

Objective(s): The students will:
— describe situations in which they felt happy.
— verbalize positive feelings.

Directions: **Review the sharing circle rules:** Go over the rules one at a time. After you have explained each rule, ask the students if they will follow it.

State the topic. In your own words, tell the students: *Sometimes we feel happy and sometimes we don't—we feel unhappy. Today we are going to talk about happy feelings in our sharing circle. The topic is, "A Time I Felt Happy."*

Can you remember a time when you felt happy? Maybe something very nice happened and you felt good about it. Or perhaps someone did something for you that you really liked. Let's close our eyes and see if we can remember a time like that, okay? Think about it and when you look up at me, I'll know that you are ready to talk and listen. I'll say the topic again. It is, "A Time I Felt Happy."

Involve the students. If no one is ready to speak, take your turn first. Then ask who would like to speak next. As the students share, model good listening by giving them your full attention. Thank each child when he or she is finished contributing.

Summary questions:
— *What kinds of things caused us to feel happy?*
— *Why is it important to tell one another about times we felt happy?*
— *How do you feel when you remember times you felt happy?*

A Time I Felt Unhappy

A Sharing Circle

Relates to:	Language Arts (oral language)
Objective(s):	The students will: — describe times when they experienced negative feelings. — state that it is normal to feel unhappy at times.
Directions:	**Review the sharing circle rules.** After the students have formed a circle, ask if they remember the sharing circle rules. Review the rules with the students and, as each rule is mentioned, ask the students if they will follow it. **State the topic.** In your own words, tell the students: *Our topic for today is, "A Time I Felt Unhappy." Everybody feels happy at times and everybody feels unhappy at other times. It's more fun for most people to tell about happy feelings, but sometimes it does us good to talk about unhappy feelings as well. Can you remember a time when you felt unhappy? Maybe you had an accident and got hurt, or perhaps you wanted something and you didn't get it so you were disappointed. If you would like to take a turn, tell us what made you unhappy and describe what the feeling was like for you, okay? Let's think about it for a moment. Then, when you are ready to share, raise your hand. The topic is, "A Time I Felt Unhappy."* **Involve the students.** Invite the students to take turns speaking. As they share, model good listening by giving them your full attention. Thank each student who shares, and remember to take a turn yourself.
Summary questions:	*— What kinds of things caused us to feel unhappy?* *— Why is it good for us to tell one another about times we felt unhappy?* *— Why can't we be happy all the time?*

Expressing Feelings Through Haiku

Poetry Writing

Relates to:	Language Arts (writing)
Objective(s):	The students will creatively express positive and negative feelings through original haiku poetry.
Time:	approximately 45 minutes
Materials needed:	pencils, paper, and several poetry books containing haiku poems
Directions:	**Ask the students if they have ever had strong feelings, such as anger or happiness, and tried to express them in writing.** Perhaps they described their emotions in a letter to a friend, or in a diary. Allow volunteers to share their experiences with the group. Explain that one way to express feelings productively is to write about them poetically. Inform the students that one type of poetry, created a long time ago to express feelings, is **haiku**. Share several haiku poems with the students, and ask them to identify the feelings expressed in the poems. Write one or two on the board and explain: *Haiku is a form of Japanese poetry in which the writer expresses a mood, usually through something in nature. Frequently, the writer captures feelings such as loneliness, sadness, beauty, and peace in just three lines. Most haiku is written with 5 syllables in the first line, 7 syllables in the second, and 5 in the third.*

Snow falls quietly.
Covering all the city.
Loneliness returns.

Ripe watermelon.
Hidden under leaves and dirt.
My birthday surprise!

Invite the students to brainstorm feeling words. List these on the board in one column. Then ask the class to think of something in nature that could be used to represent each feeling. List the item in a second column, next to the word it symbolizes. For example, an electrical storm could represent anger, with thunder and lightning expressing explosive inner conflicts. Spring, new grass, buds on the trees, and flowers could symbolize feelings of happiness and warmth. Fear could be a tiger, or some other wild animal. Sadness might be the death of an animal due to starvation.

Have every student choose a recently experienced feeling and write a 3 line haiku poem about it. Suggest that they use the 5-7-5 syllable pattern, and include references to nature. Remind them that the poem does not have to rhyme, and that its lines need not be complete sentences. Encourage the students to use descriptive words, making use of dictionaries and thesauruses. Write a haiku poem yourself to model the process. Share it with the class.

Conclude the activity. Have the students share their poems first with a partner and then in small groups. Finally, invite volunteers to read their poems to the entire class. Publish poems in a "Haiku Feelings" book or post them on the bulletin board.

Extension: Let the students put their poems to music, transforming them into short songs. An easy way to do this is to compose identical melodies for first and third lines, and a contrasting melody for the second.

One of the Best Things That Ever Happened to Me

A Sharing Circle

Relates to:	Language Arts (oral language)
Objective(s):	The students will describe a significant event from which they derive good feelings.
Directions:	**Review the sharing circle rules.** During your first few sharing circles, take time to discuss the rules with the students in a friendly way. We suggest you make a poster of the rules and read it with the students as you explain the meaning of each rule. Display the poster in the classroom and refer to it at the beginning of each sharing circle.
	Introduce the topic: In your own words, say to the students: *Our topic for this session is, "One of the Best Things that Ever Happened to Me." Can you think of something good that happened in your life that you'd feel okay telling us about? It doesn't have to be a big event, just something that made you feel good inside. It may have happened some time ago, or perhaps it was very recent. Let's take a few silent moments to think it over. The topic is, "One of the Best Things that Ever Happened to Me."*
	Involve the students. Invite them to take turns sharing. Listen carefully to each one and guide the other students to do the same. Don't allow negative interruptions. Be sure to take a turn yourself.
Summary questions:	*—What good does it do to tell each other pleasant memories?* *—Did you find out anything new and interesting about anyone?* *—What kind of feelings did you get as you talked about something good that happened to you?*

Something That Makes Me Feel Good
A Sharing Circle

Relates to:	Language Arts (oral language)
Objective(s):	The students will describe specific circumstances under which they experience positive feelings.
Directions:	**Review the sharing circle rules.** Before beginning the circle, ask the students to go over the rules. Discuss each rule in a positive manner. If you have posted a chart of rules, refer to it during the review.

Introduce the topic: In your own words, say to the students: *Today the topic for our circle is, "Something That Makes Me Feel Good." Can you think of something that makes you feel really good? It could be a person, something that you won, a pet, an event, a special place, or a time of day. What is it about this thing that makes you happy? Describe the feelings that it gives you. Let's think about it quietly for a moment before we begin to share. The topic is, "Something That Makes Me Feel Good."*

Involve the students. Invite them to take turns sharing. Listen carefully to each person who shares and encourage all members of the circle to do the same. Show the students your appreciation by thanking them after they contribute. Don't forget to share yourself.

Summary questions:

— *What kinds of things make us feel good?*
— *Why do we feel good about different things?*
— *Why do you think it is important for us to talk about good feelings?*

Take It From the Back

Role Play and Observation

Relates to:	Drama and Language Arts (written and oral language)
Objective(s):	The students will express emotions through unlimited and limited body language.
Time:	approximately 20 minutes
Materials needed:	Three boxes or other containers: In the first box, place approximately 15 slips of paper on which you have written the names of **emotions** or moods, such as *mad, sad, furious, irate, happy*, etc. (it's OK to repeat emotions, but include as many different ones as you can). In the second box, place approximately 10 slips of paper on which you have written **body parts**, such as arms, shoulders, feet, and head (these too can be repeated). In the third box, place about 5 slips of paper on which you have written different **roles**, such as teacher, parent, coach, or bus driver.
Directions:	**In your own words, introduce the activity:** *Today you are going to have a chance to do some role playing, but you are not going to use any words. You will use only your body to get the message across. And when it's your turn to take part in a role play, you'll do it with your back to the rest of us. We will try to guess what emotion you are acting out.*
	Choose two or three volunteers for the first role play. Have them silently draw one slip from the emotion box, turn their backs to the class, and independently (and nonverbally) act out the emotion they've drawn. Ask the class to guess what emotion is being dramatized. Ask for new volunteers and do two or three more rounds like this one.
	Next, have the players draw both an emotion *and* a body part. This time when they turn their backs to the class, they must act out the emotion using *only that one body part*. Do three or four rounds in this manner, with the class guessing the emotion.

Finally, have the players draw both an emotion and a role.
If, for example, a student chooses "mad" and "grandmother,"
s/he acts out the emotion the way a grandmother might be
expected to express it.

Summary questions:

Lead a discussion. Following the activity, ask the students
several open-ended questions to help them summarize what
they have learned:

— *What was it like to try to identify emotions from the back?*
  ...from the movement of only one body part?
— *What was it like to try to express emotions with only one*
  body part?
— *Which emotions or moods were the toughest to express?*
  ...to identify?
— *What were some of the main indicators of anger? fear?*
  sadness? etc.
— *Do people express emotions differently depending on their*
  role? Explain.

Ghosts and Other Scary Creatures

Literature and Drawing

Relates to:	Language Arts (listening) and Art
Objective(s):	The students will: —symbolize a real fear by creatively illustrating it. —symbolize conquering a fear by eliminating it from a second illustration. —describe how it is possible to gain control over fears.
Time:	45 minutes
Materials needed:	a copy of *The Ghost-Eye Tree* by Bill Martin, Jr., and John Archambault, illustrated by Ted Rand, New York, Holt, 1985; white construction paper; and colored markers or crayons
Directions:	**Introduce the activity.** Begin by gathering the students around for story time. Read *The Ghost-Eye Tree*, showing the beautiful and eerie illustrations. This narrative poem tells the story of a young boy and his older sister who, while walking down a dark and lonely road on an errand for Mom one night, argue over who is afraid of the dreaded "Ghost-Eye Tree." Although the story alludes to elements of familiar fears, it is humorous and all ends well. Reread the story at least once and solicit comments from the students. Ask them why the children might have thought the tree was a ghost. Explain that it is common for children to be afraid of shadows in the dark that have scary shapes and are accompanied by frightening sounds—like the shadow of a cat in the night. **Have the students illustrate one of their *own* fears.** Explain that you want them to draw the thing that scares *them* the most in the night, or at least what they imagine that thing to be. Say: *Maybe the thing that scares you is something from a bad dream, or perhaps it is something you have seen on T.V. Picture it in your mind and draw it on a piece of paper, coloring it in the scariest colors possible.*

In a second drawing, have the students "eliminate" their fear. Invite them to draw a picture of the same scary thing, but this time draw it funny or pretty, or just not frightening anymore. Talk about ways they can change the picture to get rid of the scary parts.

As they draw, encourage the students to talk about the scary things in their pictures. Praise them for their ideas, rather than for the quality of their drawings. Ask volunteers to describe their first drawings and how they were redrawn to eliminate the scary parts.

Lead a discussion. When the students have finished their drawings, encourage them to talk about the experience. Ask these and other questions:
— *How did you feel about making scary things not scary anymore?*
— *What did it feel like to take charge over the nightmare or frightening object?*
— *How can we look at scary things differently—so they don't frighten us as much?*

A Time I Felt Scared

A Sharing Circle

Relates to:	Language Arts (oral language)
Objective(s):	The students will: —describe experiences that caused them to feel fear. —state that fear is a normal emotion.
Directions:	**Review the sharing circle rules.** Ask the students to raise their hands if they can explain one of the sharing circle rules. Let them name as many rules as they can remember, and then fill in the rest. **State the topic.** Say: *Everyone feels scared from time to time and no one likes the feeling. Today, we are going to talk about feeling afraid. The topic is, "A Time I Felt Scared."* *Can you think of a time that you were afraid? What happened to cause your fear? Were you lost? Were you around a lot of people that you didn't know? Was it the first day of school? Perhaps you felt afraid the first time you tried to swim in a pool or the ocean. Chances are there is something that makes you feel scared even now. Are you afraid of the dark? Do big dogs frighten you? Maybe you feel scared when Mommy and Daddy have an argument and yell. Close your eyes and think of one time when you felt afraid. When you look up, I'll know that you are ready to begin the sharing circle. The topic is, "A Time I Felt Scared."* **Involve the students.** Ask who would like to begin, and if none of the students wants to initiate the sharing, go ahead and be first. This will show the students that adults also experience fear. Thank the students for sharing and listening.
Summary questions:	*—How do we feel inside when we are scared?* *—What do we sometimes do when we are afraid?* *—Why is it important to talk about our fears?* *—How can we help each other handle our fears?*

I Was Afraid, But I Did It Anyway

A Sharing Circle

Relates to:	Language Arts (oral language)
Objective(s):	The students will describe situations in which they overcame fear in order to accomplish a goal.
Directions:	**Review the sharing circle rules.** Ask the students to name the rules, adding any that they fail to mention. Discuss all the rules in a positive manner, and ask everyone to agree to follow them.
	Introduce the topic. In your own words, say: *Our topic for this session is, "I Was Afraid, But I Did It Anyway." Everyone feels afraid sometimes, but there are things we need to do even if we are afraid. Maybe you were afraid the first day of school, but you walked right into class anyway. Have you ever had to go to the doctor and get a shot? You might have been really scared, but you did it anyway. Or perhaps you were afraid of going into the swimming pool to take lessons, but you did it anyway, so you could learn to swim. What about staying home alone? Have the adults in your family ever had to go somewhere and asked you to stay home and wait until they came back? You were scared, but you did it anyway. Think about how you felt inside when you had to do the thing that scared you, and think about how you felt about yourself after you did it. Were you proud? Did you feel better because you did it? Think quietly for a few minutes before we share. I'll know you are ready when you look at me. This topic is, "I Was Afraid, But I Did It Anyway."*
	Involve the students. Give each one an opportunity to speak. Listen carefully and encourage the other students to listen, too. Thank each person who shares. Remember to take a turn yourself.
Summary questions:	—*What did you learn by listening to what other children did, even though they were afraid?* —*Why do you think it is helpful for us to share about times we were afraid?* —*How does doing something important, even though you are afraid, prepare you for work in the future?*

Feelings Are OK

**You are never good or bad because of the way you feel.
Finish these sentences to tune in to your feelings.**

1. The beach makes me feel_____

2. When I think of green, I feel _____

3. I feel amused when_____

   _____

4. This morning, when I got up, I felt_____

5. Walking in mud with my bare feet makes me feel_____

6. I felt angry once when _____

   _____

7. _____ makes me feel scared.

8. Red makes me feel_____

9. On a windy day, I feel _____

10. It is _____to talk about feelings.

11. I feel small when _____

12. _____ makes me feel soft and cuddly.

13. The last time I was surprised was when_____

14. The color that makes me the happiest is_____

15. Peanut butter makes me feel_____

16. _____ is how I feel about Math.

17. _____ makes me feel big.

18. Stars make me feel_____

DEVELOPING AN ACCURATE SELF-CONCEPT

Real self-esteem results from a clear view of reality. In a positive, non-critical atmosphere, these activities allow students to articulate who they are and what characteristics they possess. The students are then encouraged to take pride in their unique qualities and attributes.

An Activity I Enjoy When I'm by Myself
A Sharing Circle

Relates to:	Language Arts (oral language)
Objective(s):	The students will identify a leisure activity and describe why it is important to them.
Directions:	**Review the sharing circle rules.** Ask each student to name one rule that helps the circle run smoothly. Add any rules that are omitted, and urge the students to observe the rules throughout the session.

Introduce the topic. In your own words, say to the students: *Today we're going to discuss things we do when we're alone. The topic is, "An Activity I Enjoy When I'm by Myself."*

What do you like to do when you're alone? Maybe you enjoy reading or putting puzzles together. Possibly you like to build elaborate constructions or perfect your video-game skills. Maybe you enjoy imagining things or listening to music. Do you write stories or poems, draw pictures, or perform science experiments? Maybe you prefer to be outdoors, riding your skateboard or bicycle, or daydreaming quietly while relaxing in a special place. Think about it for a few moments. Raise your hand to show that you are ready. The topic is, "An Activity I Enjoy When I'm by Myself."

Involve the students. Invite each one to share, and take a turn yourself. Encourage the students to listen attentively, and thank those who contribute.

Summary questions:

—*Is there one activity that seems to be a favorite with several of us?*
—*How do you feel when you are involved in your activity?*
—*How do you feel about being alone?*
—*What are some things that you can do alone that are difficult to do when other people are around?*

Something Positive About Me
A Hobby Day

Relates to:	Language Arts (oral language) and Art
Objective(s):	The students will: —identify and describe a special interest or hobby. —create a poster symbolizing a special interest or hobby. —plan and deliver a presentation about a special interest or hobby.
Time:	approximately 30 minutes each for the art and writing sessions; 1 to 2 hours for the presentations, depending upon their length
Materials needed:	child-gathered items representing an interest or hobby; pencils, rulers, lined and unlined newsprint, poster board, and colored markers
Directions:	**Conduct an informal discussion about the hobbies or special interests of the students.** First, have the students briefly share with a partner something that they are interested in or like to do. Then ask volunteers to share their special interest with the class. Expect responses such as ballet dancing, playing soccer, skateboarding, building model airplanes, collecting baseball cards or dolls, cooking, or drawing. Explain that through our special interests, we expresses positive attitudes about ourselves. We demonstrate that we are interested in learning about things or developing special talents. **Announce a few days in advance that the class will be having a "Hobby Day."** Explain that the students have two assignments: First, to design a poster and, second, to prepare a presentation or demonstration of their hobby or interest. Invite the students to gather together items such as equipment, books, special clothing, or even pictures from magazines and newspapers to use in completing these assignments.

Art session: Allow the children time in class to design a poster advertising their hobby. Offer these suggestions: *Make the poster bold and simple, using symbols or simple drawings and large block letters for the words. Sketch your ideas on unlined newsprint before drawing and writing on the poster board. So that you can make corrections easily, use pencil on the poster board before tracing and coloring with the markers.*

Writing session: To prepare for the presentation, have the children write on lined paper the main ideas they want to share about their hobbies or interests. Demonstrate how to list key words and phrases for an oral presentation by writing the main ideas about *your* hobby or special interest on the chalkboard. After writing their presentation "outline," suggest that the students practice with a partner. Encourage the partners to give each other feedback regarding the clarity and completeness of the presentation.

Hobby/Interest Day: Allow the students to set up their demonstrations in different areas of the room (or use the auditorium if it is available). Instruct them to put up their posters and display any necessary equipment. Remind the students in the "audience" that they show good listening skills when they pay close attention to the presenter and raising their hands to ask questions.

Conclude the activity. Ask the students how they feel about themselves after sharing a special interest/hobby. Acknowledge them for showing that they are interested in developing a talent or learning something new.

Extension: The students may want to make their presentations to other classes as well. This can be a fun way to enhance the confidence of the students relative to speaking in front of their peers.

Something About Me That You Wouldn't Know Unless I Told You

A Sharing Circle

Relates to:	Language Arts (oral language)
Objective(s):	The students will describe things about themselves that they would like others to know.
Directions:	**Review the sharing circle rules.** Go over the rules and discuss them pleasantly with the students before beginning the circle.
	Introduce the topic. In your own words, say to the students: *Our topic for this session is, "Something About Me That You Wouldn't Know Unless I Told You."*
	Can you curl your tongue or speak another language? Did you break your arm when you were five, or find a ten dollar bill once in the street? Have you ever run a 10K? This is a chance for you to think of something that makes you special. Don't say anything that causes you to feel uncomfortable, just something that you would like to share about yourself that we might not know. Let's think about it quietly for a minute before sharing. The topic is, "Something About Me That You Wouldn't Know Unless I Told You."
	Involve the students. Invite them to take turns speaking. Encourage attentive listening and remember to take a turn yourself.
Summary questions:	*— Why is it helpful to share with others things that they might not know about us?*
	— Why do we sometimes need encouragement to tell others about ourselves?
	— What does it mean to be unique? What are some different ways in which we are unique?

Who I Am on the Inside and Outside

Art/Container Activity

Relates to:	Art and Language Arts (oral language)
Objective(s):	The students will identify their own positive inner and outer qualities and creatively symbolize them in art.
Time:	approximately 45 minutes
Materials needed:	large cans with lids (such as coffee cans) or shoe boxes with lids, magazines, colored paper, yarn, scraps of cloth, crayons or magic markers, scissors, and white glue
Directions:	**Place the materials on large tables or at other locations where the students will be working.** Give each student a container. The students will glue an assortment of pictures from magazines, pieces of material, yarn, colored paper, and/or their own designs to the outside and inside of their containers.

Explain: *We will each decorate a container on the outside and inside to show our positive outer and inner qualities. On the outside, glue pictures, designs, and colored cloth that represent positive personal qualities that you would like to show others. Decorate the inside of the container to show some of the good inner feelings you have about yourself.*

As the students work, decorate a container yourself. Suggest that the students use pictures of kids having fun, beautiful colors or designs, and fabrics that seem to represent particular feelings or qualities. Let them be as creative as they wish, as long as their efforts are positive.

Facilitate discussion. During the activity, talk to the students about positive qualities and feelings and the kinds of pictures and designs that can be used to represent them. Ask the students to talk about their choices, acknowledging them with appreciation.

Extension: Conduct a sharing session during which the students may show their decorated containers and talk about their inner and outer qualities.

A Talent I'd Like to Develop

A Sharing Circle

Relates to:	Language Arts (oral language)
Objective(s):	The students will: —describe abilities and talents that they would like to develop. —identify specific steps they can take to begin developing their talents.
Directions:	**Review the sharing circle rules.** Before beginning the circle, ask the students to take turns naming the rules. Add any rules that the students forget to mention.
	Introduce the topic. In your own words, say to the students: *Our topic for this session is, "A Talent I'd Like to Develop." Is there a special talent or ability that you wish you could develop? Do you ever daydream about being a heart surgeon, a country western singer, a great gymnast, or a soap opera star? Maybe the talent you want to develop is one that you already possess, or maybe you just wonder sometimes what it would be like to have this ability. The talent could be in any area—art, music, science, dance, athletics, etc. Take a minute or two to think it over. The topic is, "A Talent I'd Like to Develop."*
	Involve the students. Invite them to take turns speaking. Listen carefully to each one and encourage the other circle members to do the same. Don't allow negative interruptions. Remember to take a turn yourself.
Summary questions:	—*Is talent something we're born with or something we develop?* —*If you really want to develop the talent you told us about, how could you get started?* —*Do you think most adults who are famous for their talents knew what those talents were when they were your age? How do you suppose they discovered them?*

Creating My Marvelous Monster

Art/Finger and Toe Prints

Relates to:	Art and Language Arts (oral language)
Objective(s):	The students will: —their finger and toe prints as unique and one-of-a-kind. —create whimsical "monsters" from their finger and toe prints.
Time:	approximately 45 minutes
Materials needed:	white butcher paper, watercolor stamp pads in various colors, colored magic markers, buckets of soapy water, and paper towels
Directions:	**Place a 3 foot length of butcher paper on the floor in front of each student.** Evenly distribute the stamp pads and magic markers. Fill buckets with soapy water and place them in the front or back of the room, along with the paper towels.

Explain: *We are going to make sets of finger and toe prints and use them to create marvelous monsters. First, use the magic markers to trace each hand and then each foot (without your shoes) on your large piece of paper. The tracings can face any direction and be in any position. Next, using the stamp pads, make finger and toe prints inside your traced hands and feet. Wash your hands and feet in a bucket of soapy water after using them to make prints. Dry them with the paper towels. Then make a monster out of your imprinted hands and feet using the magic markers. Add a body and head and connect all the parts in some way.*

Make sure that the students wash the first hand or foot before imprinting the next one. This prevents a lot of smudging. Also, suggest that they incorporate a variety of colors, directions, and patterns to make their monsters unique.

While the students work, facilitate discussion. Point out that, just as no two snowflakes are exactly alike, no two people in all the world have finger or toe prints exactly alike. This makes each of us unique. Talk about other qualities that make people unique and special.

Display the completed monsters on the walls for everyone to see. Suggest that the students take them home at the end of the day or week.

Special Things About Me

An Art Activity

Relates to:	Art and Language Arts (listening)
Objective(s):	The students will: —identify and symbolize happy events in their lives. —identify and symbolize things they enjoy doing, alone and with others. —identify and symbolize things they do well.
Time:	approximately 1 hour
Materials needed:	one copy of the experience sheet, "Coat of Arms" for each student; construction paper, paints, crayons, magic markers, and other art materials
Directions:	**Gather the students together and tell them:** *Today you are going to have a chance to create your own personal coat of arms. On this coat of arms, you'll draw things that make you unique and special. In olden times, knights had coats of arms painted on the shields they carried into battle. These pictures and symbols represented important beliefs and experiences the knights had, as well as the powerful families they represented. When your coat of arms is finished, you will have a chance to share it with the class."*
	Distribute the "Coat of Arms" experience sheets. Ask the students draw a picture or symbol in each of the four quadrants that expresses their feelings and thoughts about the following: —In quadrant 1, draw a happy event in your life. —In quadrant 2, express in a drawing something you like to do by yourself. —In quadrant 3, express in a drawing something you like to do with others. —In quadrant 4, express in a drawing something you are good at.
	Offer help and suggestions, as needed. Question students who are having difficulty to help them identify appropriate subjects to draw.

Facilitate a sharing and discussion. When the students are finished working, have them take turns showing their coats of arms to the class. Then ask:

—*What similarities do you see in the art we created? What differences?*
—*Why is it good to understand the traditions of other people?*
—*Why is it important that we know the things that are important to us?*

Coat of Arms

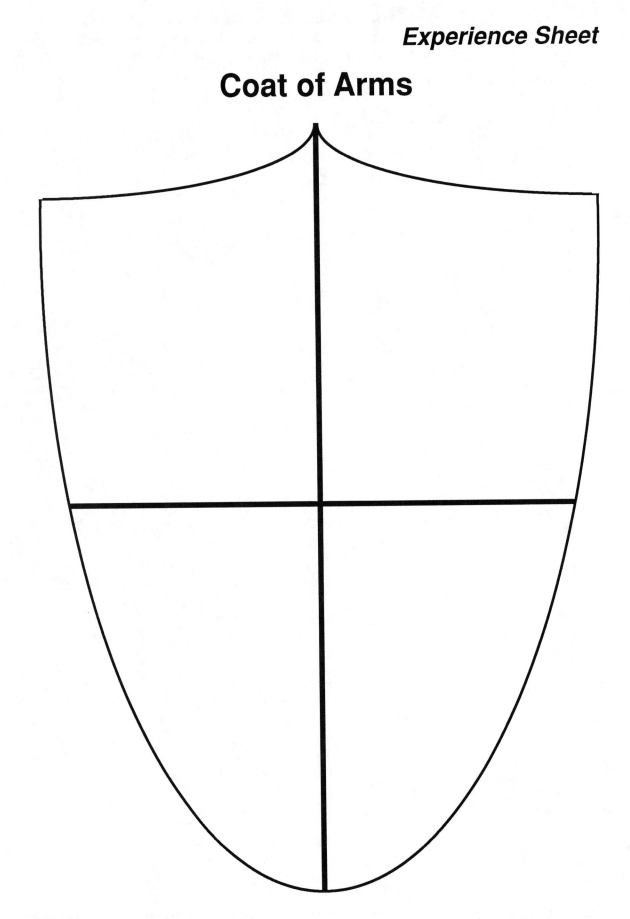

My Family: Past and Present

Experience Sheet and Discussion

Relates to:	History and Language Arts (oral and written language)
Objective(s):	The students will complete a family tree, identifying family members and their relationships.
Time:	approximately 20 minutes of class time
Materials needed:	a copy of the experience sheet, "My Family: Past and Present" for each student
Directions:	**Define for the students the term** *family tree*. You might want to show the students a diagram of your own family tree as an example. Point out that just as trees have roots and branches, so do families. One way to learn more about one's cultural heritage (roots) is to do a family tree.

Distribute the experience sheets. Ask the students to fill in the blanks on their family trees with as many names as they can remember.

Have the students take their trees home and complete them with the assistance of their parents. Suggest that they ask for information about the lives of some of their relatives. When they bring their completed family trees back to class the next day, have the students share what they have learned.

Display the family trees around the room or on a bulletin board display.

Note: Teachers need to be sensitive to the fact that some students are adopted, in foster care, or live in a non-traditional family setting. Help those students complete their family trees with people who are in their lives. Explain that culture is something we learn from those around us—not something we are born with.

My Family Past and Present

Just as trees have roots and branches, so do families. One way to learn more about your cultural heritage (roots) is to do a family tree.

Start by filling in as many names as you know in the blanks on the family tree. If you were adopted it doesn't matter. Just fill in the names of your adopted parents and their parents. Culture is something we learn, we aren't born with it.

If you know the names of ancestors who go even further back, write as many as you can above the top branches of the tree. Ask someone at home to help you!

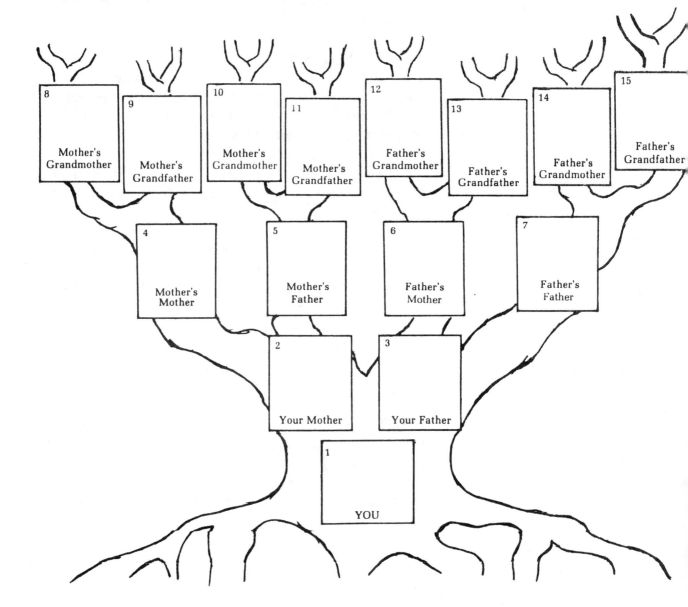

BECOMING AWARE OF STRENGTHS; ACCEPTING WEAKNESSES

Understanding that everyone has strengths and weaknesses is essential to self-acceptance and acceptance of others. These activities offer students the opportunity to non-judgmentally identify and matter-of-factly discuss their own strengths and weaknesses.

Something I Am Good At

A Sharing Circle

Relates to:	Language Arts (oral language)
Objective(s):	The students will identify and describe personal strengths.
Directions:	**As needed, review the sharing circle rules.**

Introduce the topic. In your own words, say to the students: *Our topic for this session is, "Something I Am Good At." In our circle today we are going to tell each other about things we are good at, things we do well. Some people feel they are bragging if they talk about their strengths. But it is okay to feel good about what we do well and to tell others about it. You may want to tell us about a skill you perform well in sports, or about something you are good at in school, such as math or writing. Perhaps you play a musical instrument well, or maybe you're good at being a loyal friend or a helpful person. Take a few moments to think it over. The topic is, "Something I Am Good At."*

Involve the students. Invite them to take turns speaking. Listen carefully to each person and encourage the other students to do the same. Don't allow negative interruptions. Be sure to take a turn yourself.

Summary questions:

—*How do you feel when talking about things you are good at?*
—*Is there someone you would like to get to know better based on what you heard in the circle?*
—*Why is it important to know what our strengths are?*

Something I'd Like To Do Better

A Sharing Circle

Relates to:	Language Arts (oral language)
Objective(s):	The students will identify and describe areas in which they need to improve.
Directions:	**As necessary, review the sharing circle rules.**
	Introduce the topic. In your own words, say to the students: *Our topic for this session is, "Something I'd Like To Do Better." In our circle today, we are going to tell each other about a skill or ability that we would like to improve. Think of something that you are not as good at as you would like to be. It might be some area of your school work. It might be in sports or an area of recreation. It might be the way in which you get along with members of your family or with friends. Think about it for a minute or two before we begin to share. Our circle topic is, "Something I'd Like To Do Better."*
	Involve the students. Invite them to take turns speaking. Model effective listening by giving each person your full attention. Don't allow negative interruptions. Be sure to take a turn yourself.
Summary questions:	—*Which was harder to talk about, yesterday's topic on things you do well, or today's topic on things you don't do as well as you'd like to? Why?* —*How were we different or the same in the things they want to improve?* —*Why is it important to identify the areas in which we need to improve?*

Sun/Shadow Mandala

Self-Appraisal Through Poetry Writing

Relates to:	Language Arts (writing)
Objective(s):	The students will identify their strong and weak attributes and verbalize them in poetry form on a mandala-shaped template.
Note:	This activity follows well the two sharing circles, "Something I Am Good At" and "Something I Would Like To Do Better ."
Time:	approximately 30 minutes
Materials needed:	pencils, writing paper, 12-inch by 18-inch art paper, compasses, thin point markers, yellow and grey crayons
Directions:	**Facilitate a discussion concerning specific strengths that the students have demonstrated in school subjects, home activities, athletics, games, and other areas.** Then brainstorm areas in which they would like to improve. Be sure NOT to label the second category "weaknesses," because of the negativity attached to the concept. Suggest that students who participated in the two sharing circles mentioned above (see **Note:**), think back and try to remember what they identified as strengths and improvement areas on those occasions.
	Next, instruct the students to write "Strengths" at the top of their paper. Tell them to list as many of their strengths as they can in 5 minutes. For example, a student might write: *helpful at home, friendly, pleasant, fast runner, good Nintendo player, great at multiplication, even handwriting, can whistle well, etc.*
	On the other side of the paper, have the students write the heading, "Areas for Improvement." Again, tell them to list as many specific areas of improvement as they can in 5 minutes.
	Announce that you are going to show the students how to create a very special poem and art form using the ideas they put down on their papers.

Draw a circle on the board. Explain that the circle is an ancient symbol known as the mandala. The mandala was used by several cultures, such as the Hindus and Bhuddists. Make an S inside the circle to divide it evenly into 2 curved shapes. Shade in one side with chalk, to make a distinction between the "sun," or bright side, and "shadow," or shaded side. Students may recognize this as a popular surfing company logo or the Chinese yin and yang symbol.

Explain that it is now a template for a sun/shadow mandala poem. Words and phrases indicating "strengths" are listed on the light (sun) side and "Areas for Improvement" are listed on the shaded (shadow) side. With an equal number of words on each side the mandala poem is complete.

Distribute the drawing paper, compasses, and markers. Using a compass, demonstrate how to draw a circle as large as the paper will accommodate. Then show the students how to make a large S dividing the circle into 2 equal shapes. (For younger children, make circle and S-curve templates and let the children trace them.)

Next, ask the students to write their strength words on the left side of the mandala and the improvement words on the right. Explain that there should be equal numbers of each and that they should be written side-by-side in the circle. After the poems are printed on the template, have the students color the sun/strength side yellow and the shadow/improvement side gray. The students will have created personalized sun/shadow mandala poems.

Conclude the activity. Invite each child to read his/her poem to the class, and then place the poem on a special bulletin board.

Something I Created

A Sharing Circle

Relates to:	Language Arts (oral language)
Objective(s):	The students will describe specific inventions or creative endeavors.
Directions:	**As necessary, review the sharing circle rules.** **Introduce the topic.** *Our topic for this session is, "Something I Created." Can you think of a time when you created or invented something completely new or uniquely your own? It might have been a piece of artwork, or a Halloween costume, or the decorations on a cake. Perhaps you invented a new trick to do on your bike or skateboard. Or maybe you thought of a new strategy for winning a video game. Your creation could be anything as small as a cure for hiccoughs to as large as a prize-winning short story. Let's take a few moments to think about it. The topic is, "Something I Created."* **Involve the students.** Invite them to take turns speaking, and encourage them to listen carefully to each speaker. Don't allow negative interruptions. Remember to take a turn yourself.
Summary questions:	*— How do you feel when you create or invent something?* *— Maybe doing something creative is the best way to experience a natural high. What do you think?* *— How could we be more creative, more of the time?*

My Favorite Subject at School

A Sharing Circle

Relates to:	Language Arts (oral language)
Objective(s):	The students will: — identify personal strengths in academic areas. — describe what they like about their favorite school subject.
Directions:	**As necessary, review the sharing circle rules.** **Introduce the topic.** In your own words, say to the students: *Today we're going to talk about what we most like to study. The topic is, "My Favorite Subject at School." Do you have a favorite subject at school? Is it one that is easier for you than others—one in which you get good grades? Or is it a subject that you don't know a lot about yet, but are eager to learn? Maybe your favorite subject changes each year; then again, maybe you always seem to prefer the same one. Tell us what you like about the subject, and how you feel about yourself when you are learning it. Does your favorite subject have anything to do with what you might want to be when you grow up? Think about it silently for a minute, and then we will begin to share. The topic is, "My Favorite Subject at School."* **Involve the students.** Invite each one to take a turn speaking. Listen carefully and attentively to the person talking and encourage the other students to do the same. Show the students that you appreciate their contributions by thanking them. Remember to take a turn yourself.
Summary questions:	*— What are some of the thoughts and feelings we have about our favorite subjects?* *— How do you think your favorite subject will help you become what you want to be in the future?* *— Why are some subjects favored over others?*

And the Winner Is . . .

Art/Awards Ceremony

Relates to:	Art and Language Arts (oral language)
Objective(s):	The students will: —identify accomplishments or traits for which they believe they deserve recognition. —create and present awards to each other.
Time:	approximately 40 minutes to make the awards, and 20 minutes for the ceremony
Materials needed:	magic markers, Styrofoam cups and balls, toothpicks, wide ribbon, glue, scissors, glitter, stars, construction paper, and other supplies with which to make awards (Some of the materials may be brought by the students.)
Directions:	**Place the materials on a large workspace.** Tell the students that they are going to create special awards for some very deserving people. **Explain:** *Pair up with one other person, and tell him or her about an award you really want to receive. It might be the "Big Brother/Sister Award," for all the caretaking that you do, or the "Pet Owner of the Year" award, or the "Athlete of the Year" award—for making a great play in a game. It can be any award you want to receive for something that you have done in the past. Tell your partner why you deserve this award. Your partner will then make an award for you, and present it to you later, at the Awards Ceremony. When you receive your award, you may simply say "thank you," or you may give a short acceptance speech. You may not put yourself down or discount your accomplishment in any way.* **While the students work, offer suggestions.** Help with titles for the awards, if necessary. As an example, tell the students what kind of award *you* would like to receive. **Hold an Awards Ceremony.** Act as the Master of Ceremonies for the event. Call each of the presenters and recipients forward. After each award is given, get the other students to stand and cheer. Keep it light and fun, but model serious appreciation of each student's accomplishments.

This One's for You . . .

Field Trip and Debrief

Relates to:	Art and Language Arts (oral language)
Objective(s):	The students will: —interview senior citizens and identify accomplishments and traits for which the seniors wish to be recognized. —create and present awards to the senior citizens.
Time:	approximately 1 to 3 hours
Materials needed:	award-making supplies similar to those listed in the previous activity
Directions:	**Preparation:** In this activity, the students will visit residents of a retirement home, interview them regarding their accomplishments, and present them with awards. Most communities have one or more retirement homes. Select one by looking in the yellow pages under "Retirement," "Life Care Communities," or "Homes." Call the home and speak to the director. Explain what the students will be doing. **Announce to the students in advance that they will be visiting a home where elderly people reside.** Each student will interview one of the residents, make that person an award, and then present the award at a ceremony—just as they did for each other in the activity, "And the Winner Is . . ." Make transportation arrangements, and recruit adult volunteers. **Day of the trip:** Make sure that adult volunteers know which students they are responsible for. Caution the students that some of the residents may be hard of hearing or in poor physical health. Go to the home and celebrate the accomplishments of the senior citizens. Be sure to have ample celebration supplies with you. **Lead a follow-up discussion.** During the next class session, ask the students: —*How was this award ceremony different from our own?* —*How do you think the recipients felt about their awards?* —*What did you like best about celebrating the accomplishments of others?*

One of My Best Habits

A Sharing Circle

Relates to:	Language Arts (oral language)
Objective(s):	The students will identify and describe positive habits they have developed.
Time:	approximately 15 to 20 minutes.
Directions:	**Review the sharing circle rules.** Ask the students to recall the rules that were discussed in previous circles. Review each rule with the students again, and ask them to follow it.
	Introduce the topic. In your own words, tell the students: *In our circle today, we're going to talk about good habits we've developed. The topic is, "One of My Best Habits." What good habits do you have? Maybe you do something every single day for your health, like brush your teeth. Or maybe you have the good habit of always making sure you are on time for school and other places you are supposed to be. Perhaps you make it a habit to do things to keep your life organized and smooth-running, like putting your things where they belong at home. Tell us about any good habit that you have developed. Let's think about it for a moment. Then, when you are ready to share, raise your hand. The topic is, "One of My Best Habits."*
	Involve the students. Invite them to take turns sharing. Model good listening by giving each one your full attention. Remember to take your own turn. Thank the students for participating.
Summary questions:	—*How do good habits cause us to feel about ourselves?* —*Did you get any ideas for good habits you'd like to start developing in yourself?* —*You don't have to tell us what it is, but did you realize that you might have a bad habit or two that you'd like to change?*

Good Habits; Bad Habits
Role Playing and Discussion

Relates to:	Drama and Language Arts (oral language)
Objective(s):	The students will: —identify and demonstrate good and bad habits. —describe how a bad habit can be replaced by a good one.
Time:	approximately 30 minutes.
Directions:	**Introduce the activity.** In your own words suggest to the students: *Today, let's act out and show one another some of our habits. Let's dramatize and talk about both good habits and bad ones.*

On the chalkboard, under the heading, "Good Habits," write down at least three positive habits the children name. Then do the same under the heading, "Bad Habits."

Demonstrate the role-playing process. Ask the students which habit they would like to see you dramatize. If other "actors" are needed, ask volunteers to assist you. For example, if you are demonstrating the habit of good listening, you will need to have one of the students talk to you so that you can listen. Plan the dramatization so that it will be a group effort, with you taking primary responsibility for it. Then act it out. Afterward, ask the students: *What do you think of my habit? How does it affect other people? How does it affect me?*

Ask volunteers to act out the remainder of the good and bad habits. Alternate between the two lists.

With suggestions from the students, help the volunteers plan their dramatizations. Tell them to play themselves having the habits they choose. Then allow them to enact their scenes. (Expect hilarity when the bad habits are enacted.) After each dramatization, ask the class the same discussion questions you asked after your demonstration.

Lead a summary discussion. After all of the dramatizations have been completed and discussed, ask the students:

— *What makes a good habit good?*
— *What makes a bad habit bad?*
— *How can you replace a bad habit with a good one?*

Help the students understand that good habits are not good— and bad habits are not bad—just because someone says they were good or bad. Good ones are good because they make life better for the individual who has them and/or for people that individual interacts with. Bad ones are bad because they make life difficult for the person who has them and/or for those with whom that person interacts.

Bad habits can be changed if the person with the habit:
• is able to admit that he or she has it.
• decides to replace it with a new, good habit.
• really wants to change.
• practices the new habit until the old one has been extinguished.

Three-Step Plan for Success

Improving on a Weakness

Relates to:	Language arts (oral language and writing)
Objective(s):	The children will: —identify personal strengths and weaknesses in academic areas. —formulate a plan for improving in an area of weakness.
Time:	approximately 30 minutes
Materials needed:	one copy of the experience sheet, "Three-Step Plan for Success," for each student; pencils and writing paper
Directions:	Distribute the pencils and paper. Have the students write the heading, **"Things I Am Good At in School,"** at the top of their paper. Ask them to list three *specific* things under this heading. Suggest that they avoid naming general subjects. Explain: *Rather than simply saying that you are good at Math and Writing, for example, you might say that you are very good at recalling the multiplication tables and writing poems. Or you might say that you are good at conducting science experiments, naming the characteristics of mammals, estimating, counting money, giving oral reports, or reading mysteries.* Below the first list, have the students write a second heading, **"Things I Need to Improve On in School."** Again, suggest that they list three specific items. **Distribute the experience sheets.** Tell the students that you want them to write an "action plan" for one of the items on their improvement list. Have them pick an item, and write in the name of the item to complete the heading, **"My Plan for Improving in_____"**

Step 1: Have the students choose partners. Explain that you want them to brainstorm specific ways that each of them can obtain help in his or her area of improvement. Say to them: *If you need to work on punctuation, maybe you can ask a student who is good at punctuation to work with you twice a week during recess. If you need to improve your spelling, maybe you can ask a parent or older brother or sister to quiz you at home. Write down all the alternatives you come up with under the subheading, "How I Can Get Help."*

Step 2: Point out that to improve their skill, the students will have to practice. Instruct the partners to again brainstorm alternatives and list them under the subheading, "Where and When I Will Practice My New Skill."

Step 3: Finally, ask the students to list the names of people to whom they might demonstrate their improved skill under the subheading, "To Whom I Will Show Off My New Skill."

When the three-step action plans are complete, ask volunteers to share their plans with the class. Pause at each step of a given action plan and invite the class to make additional suggestions. In this way, the students will be sure to have several alternatives to choose from. Even those who prefer not to share can benefit from listening to suggestions given to others, and will obtain new ideas for their own plans.

Challenge the students to put their improvement plans into action and report in a week on any progress made or obstacles encountered.

Lead a discussion. Encourage the students to talk about what they learned from the activity. Ask these and other open-ended questions:
—*How do you feel when you perform well in an area of study at school?*
—*How do you feel about improving in an area of weakness?*
—*How do you feel about getting help?*
—*Why is it important to make a plan of action when we want to improve in an area that is difficult?*

Three-Step Plan for Success

My Plan for Improving in _____

_____

How I Can Get Help:

_____

_____

_____

_____

_____

Where and When I Will Practice My New Skill:

_____

_____

_____

_____

To Whom I Will Show Off My New Skill:

_____

_____

_____

_____

ENHANCING SELF-TALK

The activities in this segment assist students to understand that they are constantly communicating their self-estimates to themselves, for better or worse. From this realization, students are invited to embark on a program to end negative self-talk and begin communicating with themselves in realistic, nurturing, and encouraging ways.

It's OK to Like Yourself

Teacher Presentation and Group Discussion

Relates to:	Language Arts (oral language)
Objective(s):	The students will: — evaluate the self-concepts of three fictional children based on their behaviors. — identify esteem of self as a prerequisite to esteeming others.
Time:	approximately 10 minutes.
Directions:	**Introduce the activity.** Gather the students together and tell them that you want to discuss a very important matter with them. Explain: *I want to tell you about three children who are your age. As you listen to these descriptions, see if you can tell whether or not these children like themselves.* **In your own words, present the following three character sketches: *** *Brian: The first thing people notice about Brian is his friendliness. He likes talking to everybody in his class, and to adults, too. When you talk to Brian, he listens. He frequently jokes and plays around in enjoyable ways. Brian thinks people are fun and almost everybody likes him a lot. Brian usually has a smile, but at times he becomes sad, angry, or scared of something. He isn't the smartest boy in his class, but he learns well. He isn't the best looking either.* *Carrie: The first thing people notice about Carrie is that she doesn't have much to say to most people. She acts as if her classmates aren't as good as she is. She does like two other girls in her class, and so she talks to them. She also likes her teacher. She talks to him, but not to most other adults. Carrie rarely shows how she is feeling. She hardly ever laughs and almost always seems bored. She is very smart and very pretty.*

Joe: The first thing people notice about Joe is that he is a good looking boy. Then they notice that he usually doesn't speak in a normal voice. He shouts. He shouts orders and put-downs at other children. Joe acts as though he would fight anyone who did anything to bother him. It's easy to tell how Joe is feeling, and most of the time he seems to feel like he's in charge. Like Brian, Joe is not the best student in the class, but when he pays attention and tries, he does well with all of his subjects.

Encourage the students to discuss the characters by asking:
— *Which of these children do you think really likes himself or herself?*
— *How can you tell?*
— *How does someone like Carrie who acts superior to others probably feel about herself deep inside?*
— *How does someone like Joe who acts as if he has the right to boss other people around probably feel about himself?*
— *Why do people like Brian so much? Does it help that he likes himself?*

After the students respond, suggest this point of view: *Brian really likes himself. Because he likes himself, he is able to like other people and treat them well. Carrie and Joe probably act superior and bossy because they don't like themselves very much and are trying their best to hide it. One of the reasons Brian is attractive to others is that he likes himself.*

Add the following key point: Sometimes people don't realize that it's okay to like themselves. It's not only okay, it's a necessary part of being fully happy and getting along well with others.

* Change the names of the characters, if necessary. Avoid using the names of children whom your students know.

Something I Like About Myself
A Sharing Circle

Relates to:	Language Arts (oral language)
Objective(s):	The students will identify things about themselves that they like.
Directions:	As necessary, review the sharing circle rules.

Introduce the topic. In your own words, say to the students: *Our topic for this circle is, "Something I Like About Myself." Often, we see things in ourselves that we don't like. So let's turn that around and think positively about ourselves. What is there about being you that you especially like? Your hair color? Your height? Your voice? Maybe you like the way you laugh or how gentle you are with animals. Can you read, shoot baskets, or draw well? Think about it silently for a minute before sharing. The topic is, "Something I Like About Myself."*

Involve the students. Invite each person to take a turn speaking while everyone else listens carefully, without interrupting. Be sure to take a turn yourself.

Summary questions:
—*Were we able to think of things that we like about ourselves? How were those things alike or different?*
—*Why is it important to look at ourselves in positive ways?*
—*How do the things you do well contribute to your uniqueness?*

No Time To Be Modest

An Art Activity

Relates to:	Language Arts (writing and listening) and Art
Objective(s):	The students will write positive present-tense statements about themselves expressing qualities/abilities they want to possess.
Time:	approximately 20 minutes
Materials needed:	poster paper and magic markers in various colors
Directions:	**Explain to the students that positive self-talk consists of encouraging words that we say to ourselves.** These words help us succeed. Encouraging words are powerful, particularly when we put them into positive statements about ourselves. They can bolster our spirits when we are feeling discouraged or have some negative thoughts about being able to accomplish something.

In your own words, explain: *Think of three strong, positive statements about yourself, such as "I am a good athlete," "I am very smart," or "I am a great listener." Your statements should be about things that you want to <u>become</u> skillful at— rather than things you are <u>already</u> skillful at.*

Pass out the materials, and have the students write their statements in large letters on the poster paper. Tell them to use the magic markers to make their statements colorful and decorative. Prepare a statement yourself to show as an example. Suggest that the students take their statements home and place them on a wall, or in another location where they will see them often. Tell them that each time they look at their statements, they will become more like them.

While they work, talk to the students about encouraging words, and how they can help us become more positive and capable. Assist any students who get stuck, or inadvertently include something negative in their statements. Reinforce the students for the positive statements they make. Point out that although sometimes we're told it's impolite or conceited to say good things about ourselves, these encouraging statements are not like that. They are to help the us do things we want to do.

Winning Qualities People See in Me

A Sharing Circle

Relates to:	Language Arts (oral language)
Objective(s):	The students will describe positive characteristics about themselves as perceived by others.
Directions:	**Review the sharing circle rules.** Ask the students to name the rules of the circle and commit to following them throughout the session.
	Introduce the topic. In your own words, tell the students: *Today we're going to talk about positive characteristics that others appreciate in us. Our topic is, "Winning Qualities People See in Me." Try to remember times when people have described things about you that they like, and hearing their words gave you good feelings. Maybe one of your parents recently complimented you for being reliable, or helpful, or hard-working, and you felt appreciated. Or perhaps one of your friends told you that you are fun to be with, or smart, or creative, and you really enjoyed hearing that. The compliment could have come from a teacher, relative, neighbor, or even someone you don't know very well. Close your eyes and think of a time like this and remember how you felt. Raise your hand when you are ready to speak. The topic is, "Winning Qualities People See in Me!"*
	Involve the students. Ask if anyone is ready to share. If none of the students demonstrates readiness, take your own turn. Then invite them again. Model good listening by giving each person your full attention.
Summary questions:	*—What is a winning quality?* *—Why do people like—and need—compliments?* *—Why is liking yourself so very important?* *—What can happen when people don't like themselves?*

A Time I Knew I Could Do It

A Sharing Circle

Relates to:	Language Arts (oral language)
Objective(s):	The students will describe occasions when they felt confident of their ability to accomplish specific tasks or challenges.
Directions:	**Review the sharing circle rules.** Ask the students to take turns naming the rules. Discuss any that they have had difficulty observing in previous sessions.

Introduce the topic. In your own words, say to the students: *Our topic for this session is, "A Time I Knew I Could Do It." Sometimes we just know we can do something. We don't doubt it at all. Think of a time when you felt confident that you could do something. It might have been that you knew you could master a new dance step, pass a test, sink a basket, or get your room clean before you went to the movies. It could have been something quick and easy that required limited effort, or something more difficult. Whatever it was, you knew you could do it—and you were right. Take a few moments to think it over. The topic is, "A Time I Knew I Could Do It."*

Involve the students. You might want to share first this time. Then invite the students to take turns speaking. Listen carefully, and thank each person for sharing. Don't allow negative interruptions.

Summary questions:
—How did you know that you could do the thing you shared?
—How does having confident feelings help you succeed?
—What can you do to create confident feelings in yourself?

I Succeeded Because I Encouraged Myself

A Sharing Circle

Relates to:	Language Arts (oral language)
Objective(s):	The students will: —identify a personal success. —describe how self-encouragement helps promote success.
Directions:	**Review the sharing circle rules.** Ask the students to see how many of the ground rules they can remember. Elicit responses until all of the ground rules have been mentioned. **Introduce the topic.** In your own words, say to the students: *Our topic for this session is, "I Succeeded Because I Encouraged Myself." Have you ever wanted to do something and weren't quite sure you could? Think of a time when you felt unsure, but encouraged yourself and, consequently, found a way to be successful. Perhaps you tried to teach your pet a trick, or needed to do a good job on a report for school. Maybe you were trying to master something on a computer, or were learning a new game. Whatever it was, you were not sure you could do it, but after giving yourself some encouraging words, you were successful. Take a few quiet moments to think it over. The topic is, "I Succeeded Because I Encouraged Myself."* **Involve the students.** Invite them to take turns speaking. Listen attentively and thank each person who shares. Be sure to take a turn yourself.
Summary questions:	*—What do you think caused each of you to be successful?* *—What kinds of doubts did you have to overcome to be successful?* *—What do you think would have happened if you had used discouraging words instead of encouraging words?*

My Own Gazette

Creating a Personal Newspaper

Relates to:	Language Arts (reading, writing, and oral language)
Objective(s):	The students will: — identity different parts of a newspaper. — create a newspaper about themselves, using a variety of newspaper features and components.
Time:	approximately two 1-hour sessions
Materials needed:	newspapers for each pair of students; lined paper, pencils, and white 12-inch by 18-inch drawing paper; computer(s) with word processing and page layout software, if available
Directions:	**Distribute the newspapers and ask the students (working in pairs) to scan them, identifying their component parts.** Encourage them to look first at the index and then at the different sections of the newspaper. Guide them in finding headlines, news stories, comics, classified ads, letters to the editor, sports stories, editorials, advice columns, etc. Ask several student pairs to read examples of these sections to the class. List the sections on the board and discuss the distinguishing characteristics of each.
	Explain to the students that they are going to have an opportunity to create their own newspapers about themselves. Each student will include examples of several of the newspaper parts just discussed. What will make the newspaper unique is that every part, be it news article, sports story, or editorial, will describe the student who created it. Explain to the students: *You might include a news story about something you did over a weekend, like visit a museum or participate in a church potluck dinner. In a letter to the editor, you might write about a school rule that you would like to change. You can write a classified ad describing a talent available for hire. You can create a comic strip revealing a funny experience you once had. Or a sports story describing your favorite sport or one in which you would like to excel. Other articles can describe family members and pets. Each article or feature—even*

pictures and the name of your paper—*must reveal something about you. Use names like* <u>Jenny's Journal</u>, <u>Darian's Humorous Daily</u>, <u>Cindy's Chronicle</u>, *or* <u>The Joshua Tall Times</u> *to add a personal touch.*

Have the students write rough drafts of the different parts of their personal newspapers before "publishing" them on drawing paper. (If computers and software are available, encourage as many students as possible to use them.) Suggest that students work in small groups and act as editors, proofreading one another's work before final copy is written.

Distribute drawing paper and have the students fold it vertically in half and in half again to make four columns. Younger children can fold their paper once, creating two columns. Articles can be written on lined paper and glued onto the drawing paper, or they can be written directly on the drawing paper (after editing and proofing). Allow plenty of class time. Encourage the students to work carefully in order to make their newspapers look "professional."

Conclude the activity. Post the completed newspapers on the bulletin board. Or make a booklet containing all the newspapers, and place it in the classroom or school library for all of the students to enjoy.

Dear Me . . .

A Letter-Writing Activity

Relates to:	Language Arts (writing)
Objective(s):	The students will write letters to themselves, expressing their positive qualities/abilities.
Note:	For maximum impact, do this activity *after* the students have completed the experience sheet, *Mirror, Mirror—What to Say to Yourself.*
Time:	approximately 20 minutes
Materials needed:	writing paper and pens or pencils; one envelope and one first-class postage stamp per child
Directions:	**Tell the students that they are going to write a very special letter to themselves.** They are to be exceedingly complimentary, and include all the encouraging words they can think of. The letter should contain only positive comments and remarks—nothing negative or discouraging. It should recognize their good traits, attributes, and accomplishments, and should inspire them to keep working on areas in which they want to improve. Set the tone by sharing several sample sentences with the students.
	Pass out the materials. Tell the students to begin writing. While they are working, circulate and offer assistance. Remind the students of how important their words are, and how they are affected by them. Point out that since television, newspapers, and other people at times seem to bombard us with negatives, we need all the positive input we can get.
	Have them address and stamp their envelopes. Collect the letters, and put them away in a safe place for three months. Then mail them to the students.

Mirror, Mirror—What to Say to Yourself

Sometimes other people say discouraging words to us. And sometimes, we say discouraging words to ourselves, too. When we listen to discouraging words, we begin to have doubts about ourselves. That's when we need help.

Try this:

On a <u>separate piece of paper</u>, write down 3 of the most negative things you've ever said to yourself—or that someone else has said to you.

Now rewrite those negative statements here. <u>Make them positive and encouraging.</u>
Example: *I'm just no good at math.*
Change to: *Math problems are easy and fun to solve.*

1. _____
   _____

2. _____
   _____

3. _____
   _____

Now try this:
Take the paper with the discouraging words on it, and shred it into bits. As you throw the bits of paper away, tell yourself that you are throwing away all those discouraging thought and beliefs. They are gone.

And this:
Sit in front of a mirror and repeat your positive statements aloud to yourself several times. Say them with great strength and feeling. Look yourself squarely in the eye as you speak. **Convince yourself that these things are true!**

DEVELOPING RESPONSIBILITY

Achieving competence in one's world depends upon developing responsible behavior, including the ability to effectively listen to others, understand what is heard, keep agreements, and take initiative. The activities in this segment allow the students to directly address these important challenges.

Stone Fox

Listening and Discussion

Relates to:	Language Arts (listening and oral language)
Objective(s):	The students will: —describe how work and working together can help to overcome problems. —describe positive feelings generated by helping and contributing.
Time:	as many 15- to 20-minute reading sessions as it takes to complete the book, plus one additional discussion period of approximately 20 minutes
Materials needed:	a copy of John Reynolds Gardiner's book, *Stone Fox*, illustrated by Maria Sewall (New York, Thomas Crowell, 1980). **Alternatives:** *Where the Lilies Bloom* by Vera and Bill Cleaver (Philadelphia, Lippincott, 1969); *...and Now Miguel* by Joseph Krumgold (New York, Thomas Crowell, 1953)
Directions:	**Introduce the activity.** Explain to the students that sometimes children have to work to help solve family financial problems. Ask them to think of a time when they or a young person whom they know had to help out by working. Tell them that you are going to read a book in which a ten-year-old boy does the job of an adult to help save his sick grandfather's farm. Ask them to listen to find out how he does it.
	Read the book to the students. *Stone Fox* is the story of a young boy who lives with his grandfather. He tries to keep his grandfather's farm going by hitching his dog to a plow and havesting a crop of potatoes, only to learn that they owe ten years' back taxes. The boy enters a dogsled race and stakes everything on the hope that he will win against the best racers in the country, including the legendary Stone Fox. He nearly loses the race, but is saved by his most formidable opponent.

Lead a discussion. After reading the book, ask these and other open-ended questions to help the students focus on what they learned from the story:

— *Why do you think grandfather became so ill?*

— *Why do you think little Willy took the responsibility of harvesting the potato crops with his dog, Searchlight?*

— *Why didn't little Willy accept the help of one of grandfather's friends in harvesting the crop?*

— *Why didn't little Willy want to go live with Doc Smith and let Mrs. Peacock take care of his grandfather?*

— *What would little Willy have done if he had not entered the dog sled race?*

— *Why did Stone Fox decide to help little Willy instead of winning the race and saving his own reputation?*

— *What would you have done if you were little Willy?*

— *What would you have done if you were Stone Fox?*

— *What effect does winning have on self-esteem?*

One of My Responsibilities

An Art Activity

Relates to:	Art and Language Arts (oral language)
Objective(s):	The students will creatively depict specific responsibilities they fulfill in their daily lives.
Time:	two 30-minute sessions
Materials needed:	newsprint or art paper, pencils, black construction paper, white glue, colored chalk, facial tissues, and hair spray
Directions:	**Place the materials on a table or other workspace.** Tell the students that they are going to draw one of their responsibilities with glue on black paper. After the glue dries, they will fill in the spaces with colored chalk.

Explain: *Think of one of the ways in which you are responsible and draw it with pencil on the newsprint. Your picture can show any task for which you have responsibility responsibility. For example, you might want to draw your hand holding a dog's water dish under a faucet—or yourself getting up on time in the morning. Experiment by drawing a variety of sketches. Keep your objects big and simple. When you are satisfied with a sketch, draw it on the black paper. Use the white glue to go over the pencil lines.*

Collect the drawings, and let the glue dry for several hours or overnight. It will be transparent when dry. Tell the students to fill in the shapes with colored chalk, using only one finger to spread the chalk evenly. They can clean the finger with a tissue as they change chalk colors, and wash their hands when they are done. Seal the pictures with a light coating of hair spray to keep the chalk from smearing.

As the students work, talk about those responsibilities they consider the most important. Ask them how they feel about what their pictures depict. Display the completed pictures around the room before sending them home with the students.

A Way in Which I'm Responsible

A Sharing Circle

Relates to:	Language Arts (oral language)
Objective(s):	The students will describe responsible behaviors in which they regularly engage.
Directions:	**Review the sharing circle rules.** Ask if anyone remember the rules. Allow the students to respond by stating those they can recall. Go over any that they don't mention.
	Introduce the topic. In your own words, say to the students: *The topic for today's circle is, "A Way in Which I'm Responsible." Think of a responsibility that you accept and carry out. It may be a chore that you do each week, like sweeping the kitchen floor or watering the lawn. Perhaps your responsibility is to do your homework every evening after dinner, or to read a half hour each night before bed. Maybe you get up on time every morning, or fix breakfast for yourself and your younger brothers or sisters. Do you earn and save money? That is a way of being responsible. Before we begin, think quietly for a few moments about something you do that is responsible. The topic is, "A Way in Which I'm Responsible."*
	Involve the students. Give each person an opportunity to speak. Listen carefully and encourage the other students to be attentive too. Thank each person who shares, and remember to take a turn yourself.
Summary questions:	*—What are some of the ways in which we are responsible?* *—What did you learn by hearing about what other students do that is responsible?* *—Why do you think it is important to have responsibilities?*

Trust Walk

Leadership, Exploration, and Debrief

Relates to:	Science (the senses) and Physical Education
Objective(s):	The students will: —lead a "blind" partner through a variety of experiences involving touch, smell, and hearing, and describe what that is like. —interpret stimuli from the senses (other than sight), and report the experience. —describe what it is like to be responsible for another's activities and safety.
Time:	approximately 40 minutes
Materials needed:	a large room or outdoor area that offers a variety of shapes, textures, and objects for the students to explore, by touch; blindfolds, such as scarves, dishtowels, or pieces of cloth
Directions:	**Explain to the students that this is an activity in which partners work together to build trust.** Tell them: *One partner will be blindfolded and the other will be the guide. When you are the guide, lead your "blind" partner around the room or outdoor area safely and carefully, while providing opportunities for him or her to touch different objects, listen to sounds, and smell various aromas. <u>Don't talk during the activity</u>. At the end of 10 minutes, I'll give a signal and you will change places with your partner. After 10 more minutes, I will signal you to return to the group to share what happened on your Trust Walk.* **Have the students choose partners.** Tell them to decide who will be the guide and who will be the blindfolded person during the first round. Stress the responsibility of the guides to provide a lot of experiences for their partners—but in safe ways. Also remind the students that they may not talk during the exercise. Suggest that they agree on *how* the guide will lead the partner; for example, by holding hands or by linking arms. They may establish <u>non-verbal</u> signals to indicate left, right, up, down, fast, or slow.

After each partner has had a turn to be both a blindfolded person and a guide, gather the students together for a discussion and debrief of their experiences. Ask them these questions:

— *What were some of the things you experienced on your walk?*

— *How did you feel being the guide?*

— *How did you feel being guided?*

— *What was it like to do the activity in silence?*

— *What did you learn about being responsible?*

I Helped Someone Who Needed and Wanted My Help

A Sharing Circle

Relates to:	Language Arts (oral language)
Objective(s):	The students will describe situations in which they provided assistance to others.
Directions:	**As necessary, review the sharing circle rules.** **Introduce the topic.** In your own words, say to the students: *The topic for this session is, "I Helped Someone Who Needed and Wanted My Help." Can you think of a time when you helped someone do something? Perhaps the person you helped was struggling to carry some things and you offered to take part of the load. Maybe you helped someone work on a project or a math problem that he didn't understand. Or maybe you helped someone finish a job so that the she could go somewhere, and, as a result of your assistance, the person was not only able to do the work faster, but better. Take a few moments to think it over. The topic is, "I Helped Someone Who Needed and Wanted My Help."* **Involve the students.** Invite them to take turns speaking. Listen carefully, thank each student who shares, and don't allow negative interruptions. Remember to take a turn yourself.
Summary questions:	—*What similarities were there in the things we shared?* —*How did you know the person you helped wanted your help?* —*How did you feel knowing you helped someone who needed help?*

Be Eggs-tra Careful!

Simulation and Debrief

Relates to:	Health and Safety, Art
Objective(s):	The students will: —be responsible for the 24-hour care of another (simulated). —describe what it is like to have total, continuous responsibility for the care of another.
Time:	approximately 15 minutes for preparation and 15 minutes for follow-up discussion
Materials needed:	raw eggs (one per child), and colored magic markers
Directions:	**Tell the students that they are going to have the responsibility of taking care of something very fragile and delicate for one whole day.** They will be given a raw egg to take with them everywhere they go for the next twenty-four hours.
	Give each student a raw egg. Tell the students to decorate the eggs with magic markers, making sure not to break them. Have them name their eggs, and treat them like special friends. If you like, break an egg on a plate or in a bowl, to help the students see how "heartbroken" an egg becomes when it is not properly cared for.
	Say to the students: *You must take your raw egg with you everywhere you go for the next twenty-four hours. You may set it on the table while you eat or put it on the nightstand while you sleep, but you may not hide it. It is your responsibility to protect your egg from harm and keep it company. Bring it back next time we meet, to show that you kept it safe.*
	The next time you meet, lead a discussion of the experiences the students had protecting their eggs. Ask them: —*What did you do to protect your egg during your daily activities?* —*What did you say to other people about your egg?* —*How did you feel about being in charge of something so fragile for a whole day?* —*What did you learn about being responsible while doing this activity?*

Work That's Fun!

Creative Writing and Discussion

Relates to:	Language Arts (writing, reading, and oral language)
Objective(s):	The students will: —write and illustrate stories about work activities that they enjoy. —describe how being successful requires being responsible.
Time:	approximately 30 minutes for writing, 30 minutes for editing, and 30 minutes for drawing and rewriting (may be done on consecutive days)
Materials needed:	8 1/2-inch by 11-inch writing paper; pencils; 18-inch by 24-inch sheets of drawing paper or light-colored construction paper, folded once; and crayons or colored marking pens
Directions:	**Introduce the activity.** Ask the students what kinds of work they enjoy doing at school and at home. In your own words, say: *Today, we're going to write and illustrate stories in which we are workers, doing things that we really like to do. In your story, describe what you like to do and why you like to do it. Mention any other people who help you, and name any tools you use in your work. For example, if you enjoy training your dog, write about what your dog is learning to do (and not to do), describe the collar and leash you use, and mention whether or not you take your dog to an obedience class. If anything funny has happened while you've been training your dog, describe that too. But most important, tell us <u>why</u> you enjoy working with your dog. Describe the good feelings it gives you.* **Allow time for writing.** Take a few moments to help the students identify things to write about. Then distribute the writing materials. Circulate and provide assistance to individual students.

Edit the stories. When the students are finished writing, ask them to form groups of three or four. Tell them to take turns reading their stories aloud in the group. After each reading, allow a few minutes for the other students in the group to ask questions and make suggestions about how the story could be improved. Then direct them to pass the story around so that each member of the group can help spot and correct spelling and punctuation errors.

Illustrate and rewrite the stories. Place a sheet of drawing or construction paper horizontally in front of each student, and distribute the crayons or colored marking pens. Say to the students: *Imagine that you are looking at two pages in an open book. This is called a "spread." Your story and illustration will cover this entire spread. First, decide where you want to place your story. Don't forget to allow room for a large title and your name as the author. Leave that part of the spread blank. Then draw an illustration for the story in the remaining space.*

Demonstrate by showing the students several spreads from illustrated books that you have on hand. Then circulate and help them make their layout decisions.

After the students have completed their illustrations, tell them to go ahead and rewrite their stories, with corrections, in the allotted space.

Display the completed stories around the room. Read two or three aloud to the students each day, spotlighting the author and talking to him or her about the enjoyable work described.

Something I Did to Improve Our Environment

A Sharing Circle

Relates to:	Language Arts (oral language)
Objective(s):	The students will describe ways in which they improved the environment by adding something to it or cleaning it up.
Directions:	As necessary, review the sharing circle rules.

Introduce the topic. In your own words, say to the students: *Our topic for this session is, "Something I Did to Improve Our Environment." Think of a time when you did something to improve your surroundings. It could have been picking up trash in your yard or on the school grounds, or painting over graffiti on a wall. It could have been planting a tree, pulling weeds, taking out the trash, or painting a mural on a blank wall. Improving the environment can involve either cleaning up an area, or making an area more beautiful by adding something to it. Take a few moments to think of a time when you made an improvement in one of these ways. The topic is, "Something I Did to Improve Our Environment."*

Involve the students. Invite them to take turns sharing. Listen carefully and encourage the other students to do the same. Thank each person who shares. Remember to take a turn yourself.

Summary questions:

—*Which is more fun, cleaning up an area, or adding something to beautify it? Why?*
—*What do you think would happen if we didn't do things to keep our environment clean?*
—*What are some areas you know of that could be made more attractive?*

Becoming Responsible for Others

A Look at Endangered Animals

Relates to: Science and Language Arts (reading, writing, and oral language)

Objective(s): The students will:
— research the plight of an endangered animal.
— describe humanity's responsibility to protect animals from extinction.
— demonstrate personal responsibility by helping an endangered animal.

Time: 3 to 4 sessions of about 30 minutes each

Materials needed: library books and other reference books containing information about animals currently on the endangered list; pencils, writing paper, poster paper, colored markers, paper mache or clay, tempra paint, and paint brushes

Directions: **Begin this activity with a discussion of humanity's responsibility to animals.** Talk about how humans have over-hunted animals and destroyed their habitats so that some are endangered. Get a list of the animals currently considered endangered from the local zoo or the National Wildlife Federation, Washington, D.C. Copy the list on the board, and discuss why some of the animals have been hunted to the extent that they are almost extinct. Explain, for example: *The Indian White Rhinoceros is hunted for its horn, which is said to have magical powers. In fact, the horn is composed of the same material that makes up our hair and fingernails. It is an endangered animal. Elephants are hunted for their ivory tusks and are becoming endangered. Other animals, like the leopard, are hunted for their beautiful fur, and are dwindling in numbers. The Giant Panda is endangered because humans are destroying its habitat and food supply.*

Ask that every student choose one animal to be the subject of a personal "research and help" project.

Have the students read books and magazines to gain more information on their endangered animal. Suggest that they take careful notes, which will help them explain why their animal is endangered, and will suggest ways they can aid the animal.

After the research period, have the students tell the class some of what they learned.

Ask the students to think of something they can do to help the animal. Suggest, for example: *Write a letter urging the president or government head of the country where the animal lives to do all he or she can to save the animal. Write letters to the government heads of countries where the endangered animal is hunted, and request that the hunting be stopped. Make a poster showing the endangered animal, and caption it with information about the causes of the animal's peril. Ask a local merchant to put the poster in his/her store window. Make an animal sculpture out of clay or paper mache, paint it; then place the sculpture in a shoe-box diorama showing its healthy, safe environment. Label the display and place it in the school office or library for all to see.*

Allow the students to report on their projects, and describe how they plan to help save their endangered animals. Discuss other actions they might take in the future.

Conclude the Activity. Ask the students how they feel about having assumed some responsibility for helping an endangered animal. Explain that only humans can solve the problem of animal endangerment and extinction. By taking some responsibility now, as children, they may be prepared to do even more as adults.

Response-Ability

Planning a Group Project

Relates to:	Social Studies and Language Arts (oral and written language)
Objective(s):	The students will select, plan, implement, and evaluate a class service project.
Time:	varies widely depending on project selected
Materials needed:	chart paper and magic markers
Directions:	**Remind the students of the concept of community service.** Talk with them about some of the kinds of things that they, as young people, can do to help others in the community. When you've generated some interest, suggest that the students brainstorm a list of possible projects, select one to do as a class, and develop a detailed plan for completing it.

Facilitate a brainstorming session. Stimulate creative thinking by adding some ideas yourself. For example: *collecting food to help the homeless; doing yard work for a handicapped or elderly person; planting trees; writing letters to terminally ill children; stuffing envelopes for some community organization like Hospice; visiting convalescent homes and reading to the patients; cleaning up the trash in a local park; recycling products and donating the money to a worthy cause.*

Follow these rules of brainstorming: Record all of the ideas on chart paper; don't allow evaluative comments (either positive or negative) during the brainstorming; keep the momentum going and get as many ideas down as you can.

Help the students narrow down the list by discussing the pros and cons of each suggestion. This is the time to evaluate. When the list has been pared down to just a few possibilities, select a project by consensus, if possible—by majority vote, if not.

Have the students select a project leader. Step aside and let the leader facilitate the planning of the project. From the sidelines, try to ensure that the students set up and follow a workable planning process that includes setting a goal, gathering information (through phone calls, etc.), deciding the specific steps that need to be taken to achieve the goal, appointing individuals to take those steps, and developing an accompanying timeline.

Encourage the students to be solution oriented—to think in terms of how things *can* be done rather than why they *can't* be done. Allow time for additional meetings, as necessary.

Lead a culminating discussion. When the project has been successfully completed, encourage the students to assess their work by asking:
— *What was the most rewarding aspect of the project for you?*
— *What did you learn from this project that you could use in planning another one?*
— *What did you learn about working together and helping others?*

Things I Do

Directions: Read the list of six sentences below. Each sentence describes a very important responsibility. People who *make it a habit* to do these things are almost always successful. If you make it a habit to do these things at school, there's no puzzle about it—you will be successful:

Be Positive.
Complete All Work Assigned.
Be Honest.
Be On Time.

Help Others.
Do The Best Job I Can.
Cooperate With Others.

Fill in the blank spaces below with the sentences from the list above. Some letters are already there. Use them as clues to help you complete this "very unpuzzling" puzzle.

GOAL SETTING AND ATTAINMENT

The activities in this segment emphasize the importance of establishing destinations for various segments of life's journey, including both short-term and long-range goals. As students engage in these activities, they are likely to better define personal goals and become more motivated to reach them. Several workable strategies for goal attainment are offered.

Achievement Time Capsule

Art, Collection, and Discussion

Relates to:	Art and Language arts (oral language)
Objective(s):	The students will: —make containers in which to preserve symbols of personal achievement. —describe relationships among ability, effort, and achievement. —describe positive feelings generated by achieving goals.
Time:	approximately 45 minutes
Materials needed:	one shoe box and a collection of awards and/or symbols of achievement for each student; magazines, scissors, and glue
Directions:	**Tell the students that each of them is going to have an opportunity to create a time capsule.** Explain that a time capsule is a container that holds things representing a particular period in time. Time capsules are usually sealed and stored, and are not opened again for many years. Say to the students: *This time capsule will be an <u>achievement</u> time capsule. It will remind you of your achievements at home, school, church, or in the community this year. In the time capsule, place ribbons, awards, report cards, "A" tests, programs from plays you performed in, or photographs that show you achieving something special, like diving into a pool or doing a pull-up. You might even include drawings that represent certain achievements, like planting a garden. Continue to put things into your time capsule throughout the year. At the end of the year, put the capsule away. When you open it again sometime in the future, you'll be pleased to have so many examples of your achievements.* **Distribute the materials and explain the procedure.** Say to the students: *The shoe box will become your time capsule. Decorate it with pictures from magazines. Choose pictures that represent <u>future</u> achievements. For example, if you want to become a veterinarian someday, cut out pictures of animals and paste them all over the box. If you want to achieve in sports, decorate your capsule with sports pictures. Choose a variety of pictures to represent interests, future goals, or desired achievements.*

Have a sharing session. Invite the students to share their achievement time capsules with the class. Ask them to explain why they chose certain pictures to decorate their capsule. Ask them what awards and symbols of achievement they plan to put into the time capsule during the year. Talk about the effort that will be required to realize their goals and desired achievements.

Lead a summary discussion. Ask these and other open-ended questions:
— *Why do you think it is important to talk about desired achievements?*
— *How do you feel when you achieve something?*
— *Why is it important to remember our special achievements?*

Something I Accomplished That Really Pleased Me

A Sharing Circle

Relates to:	Language Arts (oral language)
Objective(s):	The students will describe specific accomplishments from which they derived pleasure.
Directions:	**Review the sharing circle rules.** Ask who remembers the ground rules for the circle. Let the students state as many rules as they can remember. Add any that they leave out.
	Introduce the topic. In your own words, say to the students: *In the circle today, you're going to have a chance to tell us about something you did that you felt particularly good about. The topic is, "Something I Accomplished That Really Pleased Me." Maybe you got an "A" on a special report or project. Perhaps you planted something that bloomed and was beautiful. Maybe you rearranged your room, or taught someone how to do something. Whatever it was, you felt happy when you accomplished it. It's okay if the thing you tell us about was pleasing to someone else, but it must also have been pleasing to you. Think about it for a moment or two, and raise your hand when you're ready. The topic is, "Something I Accomplished That Really Pleased Me."*
	Involve the students. You might want to share first this time, making sure that you express the pleasure you felt in your accomplishment. Invite the students to take turns speaking, and thank each one for his/her contribution. Don't allow any negative interruptions.
Summary questions:	—*What was it about your accomplishment that was most pleasing?* —*What feelings were common to most of us who shared?* —*Why is it important to find pleasure in the things we accomplish?*

Shoeshine Girl

Listening and Discussion

Relates to:	Language Arts (literature and oral language)
Objective(s):	The students will: —describe relationships among ability, effort, and achievement. —identify and assess problems that interfere with attaining one's goals. —identify simple strategies used in solving problems. —describe the effects of goal attainment on self-esteem.
Time:	approximately 25 minutes
Materials needed:	a copy of the storybook, *Shoeshine Girl* by Clyde Robert Bulla, illustrated by Leigh Grant, New York, Thomas Y. Crowell, 1975
Directions:	**Read the story to the students.** Frequently invite their speculations about what will happen next, and about how they would feel if they were Sara Ida, the heroine. Sara is a young girl who wants money and takes a job at a shoeshine stand. When the owner gets hurt in an accident, Sara works extra hard to handle things herself. In the process she helps the owner, and herself, by making some money. **Lead a summary discussion.** Here are some questions to ask the students. Allow them to respond in a free-flowing manner: — *Why did Sara Ida want to go to work?* — *How good was Sara Ida at the job? How did her skill and hard work finally pay off?* — *What was the worst problem Sara Ida faced and how did she handle it?* — *What was the most interesting part of this story for you? Did it give you any good ideas?*

A Nest of Problems

Story and Discussion

Relates to:	Language Arts (reading and listening)
Objective(s):	The students will: —identify and assess problems that can interfere with attaining goals. —identify simple strategies used in solving problems. **Note:** This is the first in a series of three activities that address problem-solving and decision-making. The next two activities, "Finding a New Nest" and "What a Bear Doesn't Know about Bees" reinforce the learnings provided by this one, and broaden them to include Science.
Time:	approximately 20 to 30 minutes
Materials needed:	a copy of the story, "In Which We Are Introduced to Winnie-the-Pooh and Some Bees" from *Winnie the Pooh* by A.A. Milne, Illustrated by Ernest H. Shepard, E.P. Dutton, 1926; chart paper; and magic markers.
Directions:	**Read the story "In Which We Are Introduced to Winnie-the-Pooh and Some Bees" to the students.** The goal of Winnie-the-Pooh, in this well-known classic, is to harvest some honey from a beehive located high up in a tree. He encounters several problems in his attempt to reach the honey, and, in his own inimitable way, attempts to solve them. **As you read the story, draw attention to each problem as it is presented.** For example, when Pooh attempts to climb the tree, say: *Pooh wants to climb up and get the honey, but he's having a problem. What is Pooh's problem?* Get the students to describe how Pooh is too heavy for the branches and breaks them. Follow the same procedure for the other problems that arise—selecting the least conspicuous color balloon, navigating the balloon, arousing the suspicion of the bees, and getting the balloon back to the ground. Point out other problems that even Pooh doesn't see, such as: How can Pooh get the honey out of the hive when he's using both paws to hold tightly to the balloon?

Lead a discussion. Use these and other questions to help the students recognize and describe Pooh Bear's goal, problems, and attempted solutions. List the problems and attempted solutions on chart paper:

— *What does Pooh Bear want from the bees?*
— *What keeps him from getting the honey?*
— *How does Pooh Bear try to solve the problem of . . .?*
— *What is wrong with his solution?*
— *Pooh Bear finally gives up—do you think he should keep trying?*
— *Have you ever wanted something, but couldn't have it because a problem got in the way?*
— *How did you solve your problem?*

Conclude the activity. Thank the students for being such good listeners and for helping Pooh solve his problems. If you plan to use the other activities in this series, tell the students that they will have more opportunities to help Pooh, by learning some things about bees and beekeeping.

What a Bear Doesn't Know about Bees

Science Investigation and Art

Relates to:	Science and Art
Objective(s):	The students will: —Identify and assess problems that interfere with attaining one's goals. —Identify simple strategies used in solving problems. **Note:** This is the second in a series of three activities that address problem-solving and decision-making. Its impact is greatest when preceded by the story and discussion activity, "A Nest of Problems" and followed by the science and role-play activity, "Finding a New Nest."
Time:	approximately 30 to 40 minutes to investigate and discuss beekeeping, and 20 minutes for painting
Materials needed:	one or more books about honeybees and beekeeping technology, such as *Life of the Honeybee* by Heiderose and Andreas Fischer-Hagel, Carolrhoda Books, Minneapolis, 1986; *The Honeybee* by Paula Z. Hogan, illustrated by Geri K. Strigenz, Raintree, Milwaukee, 1979 (a particularly beautiful picture book for this age level); and/or a well-illustrated National Geographic publication or chapter from a wildlife encyclopedia
Directions:	**Remind the students of the story of Pooh Bear and the bees.** Suggest to them that if Pooh Bear wants honey—which he always does—maybe he ought to learn more about bees. And maybe they can help him. **Investigate beekeeping technology.** If you are able to locate a picture book about honeybees, read it to the students. If not, let them look at pictures from a wildlife encyclopedia or National Geographic publication while you tell them some facts about the way bees build their nests, make and use honey, air condition their hives, create queens, etc. (How bees find a place to build a new nest is the subject of the next activity.) Be sure to talk about the "cooperation" between beekeepers and honeybees—with beekeepers providing homes for colonies in

exchange for some of the honey they make. Show the students pictures of the special apparel worn by beekeepers to protect them while they are working with the hives (hat with veil, gloves) and some of the methods they use to quiet the bees so they won't sting (for example, when a small amount of smoke is released near the hive, the bees think the hive is on fire, eat all the honey they can hold to save it from being destroyed, and become sluggish and compliant in the process). Talk about beekeeping as one of many careers associated with the preservation and management of wildlife. Name others. Make appropriate charts featuring pictures, symbols, and vocabulary.

Have some of the students paint solutions to Pooh Bear's problem. Take a few minutes to brainstorm with the students ways in which Pooh Bear might be able to get the honey he wants by using actual beekeeping methods. Using temperas on butcher paper, have the students paint pictures showing Pooh Bear solving his problem by using beekeeping technology. Tell them that they can also invent other solutions, like using a firetruck boom and platform or a hovercraft.

After the paintings are dry, have each student write (or dictate) a short caption explaining his or her solution to Pooh Bear's problem. Have them use colored marking pens to letter the caption directly on the painting or on a sentence strip. Display the finished paintings and captions around the room.

Conclude the activity. Look at each painting with the students and talk about the solution pictured. Remind the students that Pooh Bear's goal was to get some honey, and that he encountered several problems trying to do it. Then draw attention to the many different kinds of solutions they came up with. Thank the students for being such good problem-solvers.

Finding a New Nest

Science Lesson and Role Play

Relates to:	Science, Drama, Movement, and Language Arts (oral language and listening)
Objective(s):	The students will: —identify simple strategies used in solving problems. —identify alternatives in decision-making situations. **Note:** This is the last in a series of three activities having to do with problem-solving and decision-making. Its impact will be greatest when preceded by the activities, "A Nest of Problems," and "What a Bear Doesn't Know about Bees."
Time:	approximately 50 minutes
Materials needed:	a copy of *The Evolution Book* by Sara Stein, Workman Publishing Company, New York, 1986; props and costume materials for the role play (optional)
Directions:	**Preparation.** Read "Househunting Honeybees" on pages 218-219 of Sara Stein's *Evolution Book*. This very short, but fascinating article describes the process by which a swarm of honeybees sets out to find a new home—usually in the cavity of a decaying tree. Every honeybee carries in its brain a "plan" for an ideal hive. A few hundred workers, each working individually, scout the countryside for likely sites. They poke into knotholes and among tree roots. When a bee finds a possible site, she checks the dimensions by pacing out the measurements from one end to the other, around the circumference, and to various points from the entrance. She returns to check the same site several times under different weather conditions and at different times of the day. Scouts come together to report their findings in the form of dances. The degree to which a site matches the "ideal" hive is reflected in the enthusiasm of the dance that is used to "sell" it to the other bees. Scouts who have less good news to report dance less vigorously, and may soon join the dance of one of the more enthusiastic bees. In so doing, they learn the location of her site, and fly off to investigate it themselves. If they like it, they return to convert still more scouts and, after several days, a decision is made.

Tell the story to the children in your own words. Simplify the language and dramatize the wonderful ability of the worker bees to achieve their goal through systematic investigation, problem-solving, and decision-making. Stress the career parallels too, e.g., that these tasks are part of the job of scout, and that the bees develop the skills to do the tasks during their first weeks of life in the nest. Demonstrate to the students the size and height of the "ideal" nest. For example, mark the minimum height of a nest (6 1/2 feet from the ground) on a wall or bulletin board, and simulate the capacity of a nest (47 quarts) by showing the children two 5-gallon bottles or some other container or space of about the right size. Involve the students in the story by asking them questions, such as:

— *Would you like to have the job of looking for a place to build a new home?*
— *Would you like to have a job that allowed you to go exploring everyday?*
— *Would you like to have a job in which you had to work alone?*

Dramatize the househunting process. Choose several students to play the part of worker bees hunting for a place to build a new nest. If you have costume materials (antennae, wings, yellow and black striped shirts, etc.) let the students wear them. While you narrate, have the scouts "fly" off in search of possible sites. If you can, have different spaces around the room available and marked for investigation. Direct each scout to measure his space by pacing it off, flying around it, etc. Have the scouts come back together and report their findings in the form of creative dances, with the most enthusiastic dances gradually gaining converts until a decision is made.

Conclude the activity. In simple language, point out to the students that the bees made their decision by 1) finding many possible sites (identifying alternatives), 2) comparing the sites to the "ideal" hive (evaluating alternatives), and 3) choosing the best site (selecting an alternative). Ask these and other questions to generate a discussion:

— *How do bees choose the best place to live?*
— *Do you think they make good decisions that way?*
— *Why is it important to look at different choices before deciding on one?*

How Did They Reach Their Goal?

Mapping a Story

Relates to:	Language Arts (reading, writing, listening, and oral language)
Objective(s):	The students will: —read (or listen to) a book in which the main character sets a goal, overcomes problems, and finally achieves the goal. —complete a story map demonstrating an understanding of the problems/solutions and sequence of events in the story.
Time:	variable reading time; about 20 to 30 minutes to complete the story map
Materials needed:	a selection of children's books in which the main character decides on a goal and works to achieve it (see selections below); pencils and writing paper
Directions:	**Invite each of your students to select a book in which a main character has a goal, overcomes obstacles and problems, and finally attains the goal.** Or select as single book to read aloud to the class. The following are excellent examples of this kind of book:

Primary

The Little Red Hen (Paul Galdone, 1973)
The King's Fountain (Lloyd Alexander, 1971)

Intermediate

East of the Sun, West of the Moon (Kathleen and Michael Hague, 1980)
By the Great Horn Spoon (Sid Fleischman, 1963)
The Trouble with Tuck (Theodore Taylor, 1981)

Upper elementary

Summer of the Monkeys (Wilson Rawls, 1980)
From the Mixed-up Files of Mrs. Basil E. Frankweiler (E.L. Konigsburg, 1968)

Allow the children sufficient time to finish reading their books. Longer books may take a few weeks to complete.

Begin the story-mapping session with a discussion. If you read a single book to the class, talk about it. If the students read independently, ask volunteers to share such things as what goal the main character set out to accomplish. Explain that in most stories, the main character runs into difficulties trying to reach his/her goal, but usually achieves the goal in the end.

Demonstrate how to make a story map. Write these headings on the board:

    Title:
    Main character(s):
    Goal(s):
    Problem:
    Solution:
    Problem:
    Solution
    (repeat this sequence as many time as there are problems/ solutions in the story)
    Final solution and attainment of goal

If you read a single book to the class, ask the students to help you complete the story map. Suggest that the students supply you with information while you write it down on the board. Then have them copy the completed map on paper.

If the students read independently, complete a sample map together. Use a simple, well-known story such as, "The Three Billy Goats Gruff." List all the problems and solutions in sequence until the goats finally cross the bridge. Then ask the students to make story maps of the books they read. When everyone is finished, invite the students to share their maps with one another in small groups.

Conclude the activity. Ask the students if the problems encountered by the main character made the story more interesting than it would have been if the character immediately got what s/he wanted. Post the story maps on the bulletin board or in the library to "advertise" the featured books.

I Made a Plan and Followed Through
A Sharing Circle

Relates to:	Language Arts (oral language)
Objective(s):	The students will describe a goal that was reached through planning and follow-through.
Directions:	**Review the sharing circle rules.** Ask volunteers to describe ground rules that they think are particularly important. Fill in any that are omitted.
	Introduce the topic. In your own words, say to the students: *Our topic for today is, "I Made a Plan and Followed Through." Think of a time when there was something you really wanted to do, and it required some planning on your part. You may have wanted a bike or a stereo, and had to save money to help pay for it. Or maybe you wanted very much to pass a test , or get an "A" in a class—and to do it, you had to plan a study schedule. Possibly you wanted to surprise someone with a party or a gift, and you had to prepare carefully to create the surprise. Whatever it was—your plan succeeded. Take a few moments to think of such a time before we share. The topic is, "I Made a Plan and Followed Through."*
	Involve the students. Invite everyone to share. If necessary, take your turn first to generate additional ideas. Thank each person who shares.
Summary questions:	—*What was similar about our plans?* —*Why do we sometimes need help to carry out our plans?* —*What do you think would have happened if no one had made a plan?* —*How was it helpful to hear about all these plans that succeeded?*

Charting an Adventure

An Action Plan

Relates to:	Social Studies and Language Arts (oral and written language)
Objective(s):	The students will: —describe an exciting experience they had or risk they took, and state the goal of the experience. —identify others who participated in the experience and describe their roles.
Time:	approximately 30 minutes
Materials needed:	one large sheet of butcher paper for each group of 5 to 6 students, and felt-tip markers
Directions:	**Preparation:** Make a chart on the chalkboard with three columns whose headings read: "Adventures," "Goals," and "How Others Helped."

Introduce the activity. Ask the students if they have had any real-life adventures. Explain that an adventure is an exciting experience that may involve risk or danger. Invite the students to tell the class about their adventures. Ask them to state what their adventure was about, the goals of the adventure, and how other people helped during the adventure. Write a few of their responses on the chart. The following are examples:

Adventure	Goals	How Others Help
Hiking up a mountain	Getting up and back	Carrying food/water; clearing the trail
Camping out in the woods	Living without modern conveniences	Setting up tent; making campfire; cooking
Bicycle race	Ride around track quickly and safely	Getting bike in shape
Earning a belt in Karate	Becoming stronger, more coordinated and flexible	Teaching the skills

Divide the class into groups of five or six. Ask each group to create a chart of adventures that the students in the group have had *or would like to have*. Ask the students to think about the goal of each adventure. Encourage them to discuss the ways in which others helped (or would help) reach the goal. After the groups have created their charts, invite them to share with the rest of the class.

Lead a culminating discussion. Ask these and other open-ended questions to help the students focus on what they learned from the activity:
—*Why is it helpful to talk about the goals of an adventure?*
—*In what ways do we cooperate with others in an adventure?*
—*How do you feel about having an adventure?*

What Do You Really, Really Want?

Art and Creative Thought

Relates to:	Art and Language Arts (written and oral language)
Objective(s):	The students will identify and pictorially describe three goals they want to achieve in their present or future life.
Time:	approximately 30 minutes
Materials needed:	three sheets of colored, notebook-size paper for each student; white glue, scissors, pens or pencils, and plenty of popular (with children) magazines
Directions:	Place the materials on large tables, dividing them evenly among the students.

Tell the students that they will be cutting out words and pictures from the magazines and gluing them to their colored sheets of paper. They can also *create* drawings and designs to supplement what they find in the magazines. Explain to the students: *I want you to make three pictures showing things that you really, really, really want to have in your life. Before you start, take a moment and think about what you would like most to have, to be, to see, or to do. Then, make a list of the <u>three</u> most important things. Cut out pictures and words that describe what you want from the magazines, and glue them to your paper. You have one sheet on which to show each thing that you want. If you like, make drawings and designs of your own, instead of cutting them from magazines.*

Circulate and assist anyone who is having difficulty. Encourage creativity. Talk with individual students about their choices. Although there is no right or wrong way to approach this activity, be sure that the desires/goals chosen by the students are positive ones.

Conclude the activity. Display the finished art work on a bulletin board. Each day, have several students show their pictures to the class, describing the goal each represents, and how they hope to attain it.

One of My Goals Is . . .

Triads and Discussion

Relates to:	Language Arts (oral language)
Objective(s):	The students will: —state specific goals and identify obstacles to achieving them. —describe ways of overcoming obstacles to goal achievement.
Time:	approximately 20 to 30 minutes
Materials needed:	Plan to use a space large enough to accommodate groups of three students, allowing ample space between groups.
Directions:	**Divide the students randomly into groups of three.** Have them decide who will be **A**, who will be **B**, and who will be **C**. (If one or two students are left over, you can assign additional **C**'s to some groups.)

Announce that the triads are going to practice dealing with obstacles to goal achievement. In your own words, explain: *Person A, you are the "goal-setter," and will state a goal that you want to achieve. Person B, you are the "discourager." You will come up with all the problems, obstacles, and roadblocks that could make achieving the goal difficult. Person C, you are the "encourager." You will offer ideas and solutions for achieving the goal. You will help* remove *the roadblocks. Offer any good ideas you can think of to help the goal-setter be successful. After a few minutes, I'll call time and tell you to switch roles.*

Choose two volunteers and demonstrate the rotation process and the goal-setter/discourager/encourager interaction. Provide examples of goal statements, positive statements, and negative statements.

Lead the activity through three rounds. Circulate, and encourage the students to play their roles with enthusiasm.

Facilitate a follow-up discussion. After everyone has had a turn in each role, gather the students together and ask them:
—*What obstacles or roadblocks were mentioned most often?*
—*What were some of the best solutions offered?*
—*Do you think this activity will help you accomplish your goals? How?*

I Am Reaching My Goal

Think of a skill or ability that you want to develop or improve. It can be related to school, hobbies, sports, friends, family, vacations—just about anything.
Describe it here:

_____
_____
_____

Now turn it into a goal. Fill in the blanks below to create a goal statement. Here are some examples: *BY June 1, I AM running 3 miles a day. BY November 15, I HAVE read and reported on 6 books. BY Saturday, I AM living in a clean bedroom, that I take care of myself.*

*BY*_____*, I AM/HAVE*

_____
_____
_____

Now, ask yourself: *How will I benefit from reaching this goal?*

_____
_____

What things might stop me from reaching this goal?	*What can I do to prevent these things from stopping me?*
_____	_____
_____	_____
_____	_____

Now, make a plan. What is the first thing you need to do to reach your goal? List it below. Put a date beside it to show when you will do it. List all other steps that you need to take to reach your goal.

STEP	DATE
_____	_____
_____	_____
_____	_____
_____	_____

Very important! Picture yourself reaching your goal—having the skill you want to have, or doing the thing you want to do. Draw that picture on the back of this paper. And picture it *in your mind* several times every day.

MANAGING STRESS

This segment focuses student attention on the fundamental importance of physical, mental and emotional health. In addition to providing important information, the activities in this segment encourage students to take conscious control of their own wellness.

Something That Causes Me Stress

A Sharing Circle

Relates to:	Language Arts (oral language)
Objective(s):	The students will identify stressors in their lives.

Review the sharing circle rules. Discuss the ground rules in a positive way, adding any that the students forget to mention.

Introduce the topic. In your own words, say to the students: *Our topic for this session is, "Something That Causes Me Stress." Do you ever get tongue tied? Feel uptight or on edge? Get a headache or a queezie stomach when you're not sick? Chances are the cause of those feelings is stress. Many different things can cause stress—worrying about a test, feeling angry at someone, or not getting enough sleep, for example. Even good things can cause stress—like the excitement of waiting for a special event. Think of something that causes you stress and tell us about it. What happens to cause the stress, and how does it affect the way you feel, the thoughts you have, and the things you do? Take a few minutes to think about it. The topic is, "Something That Causes Me Stress."*

Involve the students. Invite them to take turns speaking. Listen carefully to each person who shares, and encourage the students to do the same. Don't allow negative interruptions. Be sure to take a turn yourself.

Note: Quietly make a list of the things that cause the students stress, for use in the activity, "From Panic to Power."

Summary questions:
—*Do the same kinds of things frequently cause you stress?*
—*If you know something is likely to stress you, what can you do about it?*
—*Do feelings of stress do us any good? Explain your answer.*

From Panic to Power

Brainstorming and Discussion

Relates to:	Health and Language Arts (written and oral language)
Objective(s):	The students will: —define the term *stress*. —identify actions they can take to reduce stress in specific situations.
Time:	approximately 20 minutes
Materials needed:	chart paper and marking pen or chalkboard and chalk; the list of stressors you recorded during the sharing circle, "Something That Causes Me Stress" (optional)
Directions:	**Tell the students that the class is going to spend some time talking about stress—what it is and what can be done about it.** Begin by listing on chart paper the stressors that the students mentioned during the circle session, "Something That Causes Me Stress." Then brainstorm additional stressors to add to the list.

Define the term *stress*. For example, say: *Here's a formula that explains stress:*

STRESSOR + PHYSICAL REACTION - ACTION = STRESS.

When we think we're in danger (of failing, being embarrassed, not getting what we want, etc.), our bodies react just like they would if we were in danger of being attacked by a lion. Adrenaline and hormones start pumping, our hearts beat faster, our muscles tense, and we get set for "fight or flight." Then if we <u>don't</u> take action—if we just sit around and worry, for example— all those unused hormones and tense muscles end up hurting <u>us</u>.

Next, go through the list, one item at a time. Have the students brainstorm **actions** they could take in each situation. For example, if they don't understand the current chapter in math, they can talk to the teacher, ask a parent for help, study with a friend, etc.

Empower the students by demonstrating enthusiasm about all the things they can do. Lead them in a rousing "I Can Do It!" cheer after each item is discussed.

When the stressor is something the students have no control over (like the death of a pet) or little control over (like noisy neighbors), acknowledge that even though they can't "act on" the stressor directly, they *can* use **stress reducers**.

Act out some of the stressful situations. Concentrate on those in which the students have some control, and encourage them to take turns dramatizing the different courses of action they could take. Lead a discussion after each dramatization.

What Makes Me Mad

Reading, Discussion, and Singing

Relates to:	Language Arts (reading and oral language)
Objective(s):	The students will: —identify causes of anger. —situations in which they experienced anger. —name specific ways of alleviating feelings of anger.
Time:	approximately 20 minutes
Materials needed:	a copy of Norma Simon's book *I Was So Mad!*, illustrated by Dora Leder (Chicago, Albert Whitman, 1974)
Directions:	**Gather the students together and read them *I Was So Mad!* by Norma Simon.** The story portrays situations, from a child's perspective, that result in negative feelings like frustration, anxiety, humiliation and loss of control. It describes the inner and outer struggles of children as they try to control feelings and work them out in acceptable ways—sometimes successfully, sometimes not. The book ends with a song that one child's father sings when he gets mad and "feels like a firecracker going off."

After reading the book, conduct a discussion by asking the following questions:
— *Do you get mad when...*
Add situations from the book such as:
> ...you are the first to go to bed?
> ...someone breaks your best toy?

After getting responses to the first question, ask:
— *Who would like to give an example of a time when this happened to you?*
— *Who can think of an idea to help the mad feelings go away?*

Brainstorm ideas and guide the students to think of workable, yet appropriate, solutions.

Teach the students the song, "There Was a Man and He Was Mad." You will find it on the back of the book, *I Was So Mad!* Let the students jump when the word "jump" is repeated in all the verses.

Conclude the activity. Thank the children for sharing and listening. Tell them that sometimes just talking about their mad feelings will help them feel better.

Other books about anger:
The Hating Book by Charlotte Zolotow (New York, Harper & Row, 1969)
Boy, Was I Mad! by Kathryn Hitte (New York, Parents Magazine Press, 1969)
I'll Fix Anthony by Judith Viorst (New York, Harper & Row, 1969)
The Temper Tantrum Book by Edna Preston (New York, Viking, 1969, 1971)

What I Do When the Going Gets Tough

A Sharing Circle

Relates to:	Language Arts (oral language)
Objective(s):	The students will describe positive ways in which they handle stress.
Directions:	As necessary, review the sharing circle rules.

Introduce the topic. In your own words, say to the students: *Our topic for this session is, "What I Do When the Going Gets Tough." Most of us have ways to make ourselves feel better when we're stressed. What's one of your ways? What do you do to help yourself when you feel angry, worried, tense, or nervous? Maybe you talk to one of your parents or to a friend about what's bothering you. Or perhaps you take a long walk or bike ride. Spending time alone with your pet may make you feel better. Or perhaps you do something to take your mind off the stressful situation—like watching TV, going to a movie, or reading a book. Tell us what you do, and how you feel when you do it. Let's think it over for a few moments. The topic is, "What I Do When the Going Gets Tough."*

Involve the students. Invite them to take turns sharing. Model attentive listening, and don't allow negative interruptions. Remember to take a turn yourself.

Summary questions:

—*Why is it important to find positive ways to handle stress?*
—*What are some negative ways in which people try to handle stress?*
—*Do you think fewer people would use alcohol and drugs if they knew how to handle stress in more positive ways?*

The Comedy Show

Using Humor to Reduce Stress

Relates to:	Drama and Language Arts (oral language and listening)
Objective(s):	The students will: —create and perform funny acts. —demonstrate the benefits of laughter in reducing stress.
Time:	approximately 30 minutes for planning and 15 to 20 minutes for the show
Materials needed:	"found" materials to use as props for skits and monologues
Directions:	**Review with the students various ways to reduce stress.** Allow the students to name examples, such as specific forms of exercise, guided imagery, relaxation, playing games, and solving puzzles or problems. Inform them that laughter is another good way to reduce stress and tension. Explain: *When we create humorous situations, we can laugh at ourselves. The more we laugh, the more our muscles relax.* **Announce that the students are going to have an opportunity to create humor by participating in an informal "comedy show."** Every student will have a turn being a comedian and the rest of the time will be a member of the audience. As comedians, the students can tell jokes, read funny poetry (poems by Shel Silverstein or Jack Prelutsky are superb for this activity), enact silly skits with a group, sing funny songs, or do comical impersonations. Students can work alone, with a partner, or with a small group to plan their "act." Simple classroom furniture, yardsticks, and playground equipment can be used as props. **When the students have prepared their "acts," move the desks aside so that chairs can be placed in rows for the audience.** Make sure that there is plenty of room for a "stage." Introduce each act in turn. Encourage plenty of laughter and applause. When finished, have the performer(s) join the audience.

Lead a summary discussion. Ask the students these and other open-ended questions:

— *What feelings do you have in your body when you laugh a lot?*

— *How does laughter affect your thoughts and feelings?*

— *What was it like to create a comedy act? ...to perform it?*

— *What can you do at home to make yourself laugh?*

Four Floors of Fantasy

Using Guided Imagery to Reduce Stress

Relates to:	Health and Language Arts (listening)
Objective(s):	The students will practice using guided imagery to relieve stress.
Time:	approximately 20 minutes
Materials needed:	watch or clock with second hand; optional cassette tape player and tape of relaxing instrumental music
Directions:	**If you have music, start the tape at a low volume so that you can speak over it easily.** Use a relaxing tone of voice. Read the following passage <u>slowly</u>, pausing where indicated:

*You are going to take a ride on an imaginary elevator. Sit or lie in a comfortable position. Be sure you are not touching anyone, and remember not to talk, whisper, or move about during the exercise. Close your eyes and relax your body. Become aware of your breathing (pause 15-20 seconds). Begin counting your breath silently in your mind (pause 45-60 seconds). Now imagine that you are standing in front of an elevator door. You press the button and the door opens, showing you a large well-lighted, empty elevator. You enter it and find that the elevator buttons are labelled as follows: The first button says, "**this room;**" the second button says, "**a peaceful place;**" the third button says, "**a visit with a wise older person;**" the fourth button says, "**a super adventure;**" and the fifth button says, "**a visit with a long-lost friend.**" Choose the floor you would like to go to (pause 15 seconds), and press the button. The elevator door slowly closes and the elevator begins to rise to the floor you selected. The elevator arrives at the floor and the doors slowly open. Go out into the space and explore it. Meet whoever is there; do whatever makes sense for you to do there. (pause at least 60 seconds). Now say good-by to the place you're in, and to anyone who is there. The elevator has remained open for you. Enter it now. Take one last look at the place you have been. Press the button marked "this room." The elevator doors close and the elevator slowly returns you to this room (pause 15 seconds). As the elevator doors open, so do your eyes (pause until everyone's eyes are open). Welcome back!*

Have the students pair up. Suggest that they tell their partners as much as they would like to about their fantasies. Allow 2-3 minutes for sharing.

Lead a summary discussion. Ask these and other open-ended questions:
— *What kinds of feelings did you have during this exercise?*
— *How can you use your imagination to reduce stress?*

Stress Breaks

Using Movement to Reduce Stress

Relates to: Physical Education

Objective(s): The students will invent simple movements to relieve stress.

Time: approximately 15 minutes

Materials needed: a large circle of chairs—one chair for each child

Directions: **Ask the students to sit in a circle.** Announce that the class is going to invent and practice "stress breaks" that can be used at other times to reduce stress. In your own words, explain: *One of best things you can do to relieve stress is exercise. And that doesn't just mean running a mile or playing a basketball game—almost any kind of stretching or moving can help get the tension out of muscles and make the heart beat faster. Think of a movement that you can do sitting down. You can pump your arm up and down, roll your shoulders backwards and forwards; or "run" very fast with your feet.* (Demonstrate several sitting movements for the students.) *We're going to go around the circle and each one of you is going to lead us in a movement for 10 seconds. When it's your turn, show us a movement that <u>no one else has done</u> and we'll all do it with you.*

Get the game started and keep it going at a lively pace. Participate along with the students.

After every person has led a movement, tell the students to stand and move their chairs out of the way. Go around the circle again, this time creating movements that can be done from a **standing** position. Demonstrate a few, like running in place, stretching to the side, etc.

Finally, have each student lead a "traveling" movement for 5-10 seconds. Maintain the circle formation. Suggest that skipping, hopping, jogging, etc., can be done using different kinds of arm movements for variation.

I Like My Neighbor Who . . .

A Movement Game

Relates to:	Physical Education
Objective(s):	The students participate in a game that uses movement and creativity to relieve stress.
Time:	approximately 15 minutes
Materials needed:	moveable chairs for all but one student in your class
Directions:	This unique form of musical chairs offers an exhilarating, fun way to work off stress and excess energy.

Place the chairs in a large circle, facing inward. Direct all of the students to sit in a chair. One student will be left over. Have that person stand in the center of the circle.

Announce that exercise and a change of focus are good ways to relieve stress. Tell the students that the game they are about to play accomplishes both. In your own words, explain how it is played: *In this game, the student in the middle will say, "I like my neighbor who..." and then name some characteristic that describes any person in the circle. For example, the student may add, "is wearing a T-shirt," "has a dog," "is less than 10 years old," or "has brown eyes." The characteristic does not have to describe the person who is "It," but it must be positive and not embarrassing. As soon as the student names the characteristic, the students who are sitting down who have that characteristic must get out of their chairs and find new chairs. At the same time, the student in the middle must try to scramble for one of the empty chairs. Whoever is left without a chair is then "It."*

Before starting the game, stress the one ground rule: No Running. If the students feel like running, they must do it in slow motion. Demonstrate slow motion running, exaggerating your slow movements. The kids will imitate you and safely have fun.

Allow the game to proceed until <u>every student</u> has been "it" at least once. (Almost all people like to be in the spotlight, even if they won't admit it.)

Something I Do for Myself When I'm Sick

A Sharing Circle

Relates to:	Language Arts (oral language)
Objective(s):	The students will describe specific ways in which they take care of themselves when they are sick.
Directions:	**Review the sharing circle rules.** After the students have formed a circle, call on volunteers to state the rules. Discuss any rule that the students have had difficulty following in previous sessions.

Introduce the topic. In your own words, say to the students: *The topic for today's circle session is, "Something I Do For Myself When I'm Sick." We all get sick from time to time, and most of us have learned things that we can do to get well again. Think of times when you've been sick. What do you do to help yourself get better. Maybe you drink a lot of liquids when you have a cold, or wash off a scraped knee with soap and water before you put on a bandage. Maybe you play soft music and rest when you have a headache. Whatever it is, you do it yourself, and it helps make you better. Let's take a minute to think about it silently before we share. The topic is, "Something I Do For Myself When I'm Sick."*

Involve the students. Allow each student to have a turn speaking, and encourage attentive listening. If necessary, take a turn first, to help evoke memories in the minds of students who can't think of anything right away. Thank everyone who shares.

Summary questions:
— *How do you feel about doing something for yourself when you are sick?*
— *Why is it important to do something good for yourself when you are sick?*

A Time I Didn't Take Care of Myself and Paid the Price

A Sharing Circle

Relates to:	Language Arts (oral language)
Objective(s):	The students will describe specific consequences of not taking care of themselves.
Directions:	**As necessary, review the sharing circle rules.**
	Introduce the topic. In your own words, say to the students: *Today, the topic for our circle session is, "A Time I Didn't Take Care of Myself and Paid the Price." Can you think of a time that you really suffered because you didn't take care of yourself? Maybe you didn't brush your teeth after meals when you were younger, and then got a cavity that had to be drilled and filled by the dentist. Perhaps you cut yourself once and didn't clean the cut, so it got infected. Did you ever eat too many sweets at a party and then get sick? Have you ever stayed up so late reading or playing video games that you were too sleepy to do well on a test the next day? How did you feel about what happened? Think about it quietly for a moment. The topic is, "A Time I Didn't Take Care of Myself and Paid the Price."*
	Involve the students. Listen carefully to the person who is talking and encourage the others to do the same. Show the students your appreciation for their contributions by thanking them after they share. Remember to take a turn yourself.
Summary questions:	—*Did we have similar feelings when we suffered the consequences of not taking care of ourselves? What were they?* —*Why do you think we don't take care of ourselves sometimes?* —*If you could relive the situation you shared, what would you do differently?*

Take the Up Elevator!

Remember the elevator exercise? It was a good way to relax and get rid of stress. Now try this elevator:

Eat Right. Don't skip breakfast. Cut down on sweets. Eat something from each of the 4 food groups every day. The 4 food groups are:

1. _____ 3. _____

2. _____ 4. _____

Laugh! Tell a joke. Make a funny face. Draw it here:

Exercise! List 3 ways YOU can get regular exercise:

1. _____

2. _____

3. _____

Voice your feelings! When something's bothering you, to whom can you talk? _____

_____

Act! Think of a problem. What can you do to solve it?

_____

_____

Turn it around! If you can't solve a problem, change your feelings about it.

   Motto: *If you don't get what you want, want what you get.*

Organize! Make good use of your time. Get your work done. What can **YOU** do to be better organized? _____

_____

_____

Relax! Breath deeply. Get lots of sleep. Take the fantasy elevator to an imaginary place.

GOING UP!

DEVELOPING EFFECTIVE COMMUNICATION SKILLS

The ability to effectively communicate with others leads to satisfying life experiences which directly and indirectly affect self-esteem. These activities assist students to understand the importance of effectively communicating and allow them to practice useful interpersonal skills, including assertiveness and the use of congruent body language.

A Time I Listened Well to Someone

A Sharing Circle

Relates to:	Language Arts (oral language)
Objective(s):	The students will: —describe the importance of good listening. —identify characteristics of good listeners.
Directions:	As necessary, review the sharing circle rules.

Introduce the topic. In your own words, say to the students: *The topic for this session is, "A Time I Listened Well to Someone." We've been doing a lot of talking and sharing in our circles, and we have also been listening well to one another. If we hadn't been good listeners, our circles wouldn't have worked. Listening is just as important to communication as talking.*

Can you think of a time when you listened carefully to another person? Perhaps you had a friend who needed to talk about a problem, and you showed you cared by listening and saying very little. Or maybe it was a situation in which you learned a lot from someone who had some interesting and important things to say. Think about times like these, when you used your listening skills, and tell us about one of them. Let's take a few moments to think it over. The topic is, "A Time I Listened Well to Someone."

Involve the students. Invite them to take turns speaking. Encourage the group to listen carefully as each person shares. Don't allow negative interruptions. Be sure to take a turn yourself.

Summary questions:

—*Can you tell if someone is listening to you or not?*
—*When you know someone is listening, how do you feel?*
—*How do you feel when the person you are talking to isn't listening?*

Someone I Like to Talk With

A Sharing Circle

Relates to:	Language Arts (oral language)
Objective(s):	The students will describe characteristics of effective communicators.
Directions:	As necessary, review the sharing circle rules.

Introduce the topic. In your own words, say to the students: *Our topic for this circle is, "Someone I Like to Talk With." Being able to talk with other people is very important for all of us. Most of us find that certain people we know are easier to talk with than others. Can you think of someone with whom you enjoy having conversations? Perhaps the person you like to talk with is a good friend your own age, or a teenager—or maybe he or she is an adult. Tell us about the person and what kind of conversations you have. Let's take a few silent moments to think it over. The topic is, "Someone I Like to Talk With."*

Involve the students. Invite them to take turns speaking. Model good listening by giving each speaker your full attention. Don't allow negative interruptions. Be sure to take a turn yourself.

Summary questions:	—*Why are conversations with the people we talked about so satisfying?* —*Do all of these people have similar qualities and abilities and, if so, what are they?"* —*Is being able to speak well an important ability for each of us to develop? Why?*

That's a Fine How Do Ya Do

Verbal/Nonverbal Experiment and Discussion

Relates to:	Language Arts (oral language)
Objective(s):	The students will demonstrate a variety of verbal and nonverbal greetings.
Time:	approximately 15 minutes
Materials needed:	cassette recorder; upbeat musical tapes; an unobstructed, open space; and a watch or clock for timing
Directions:	**Set the recorder up where it will not be in the way of moving students.** Play the music throughout the activity.

In your own words, give these directions: *Mill around the room and greet as many people as you can in five minutes. Try to use different words and methods to greet each person. It's okay to say something someone else has said, but you must not use the same greeting twice.*

Tell the students to begin. Call time at the end of five minutes.

To start the second round, explain: *Mill around and greet everyone again, but this time do it nonverbally. You may use gestures, movements, facial expressions, even sounds, but you may not use words! Again, it is okay to do something that someone else has done, but don't use the same method twice. Greet everyone in the group differently.*

Tell the students to begin, and call time at the end of five minutes.

Lead a summary discussion. At the end of the experiment, call the students together and ask:
— did you feel when you couldn't use words?
— What are some nonverbal greetings you used that you had never thought of before?
— What similarities did your greetings have?
— Which method did you think was most effective—verbal or nonverbal?

Tape the Message and Play It Back
Dyads and Discussion

Relates to:	Language Arts (oral language)
Objective(s):	The students will listen to each other in dyads, and practice feeding back what they hear.
Time:	approximately 15 minutes
Directions:	**Talk with the students about how communication involves two functions: 1) giving, and 2) receiving messages.** We give messages by speaking, and we receive them by listening. In order to be effective communicators, we have to perform both functions well.

In your own words, explain: *Let's see how good we are at receiving messages. I have an activity in mind that will give us a chance to see how well we can listen. The activity is called, "Tape the Message and Play It Back." You will try to "tape record" in your mind what someone says, and then tell that person what you heard, to see if you got it right.*

Ask the students to form dyads. Have them decide who is **A** and who is **B**. Then direct them through this process:

First minute: A speaks. Topic: *What I Like About My Favorite Game*
Second minute: B "plays back" what s/he heard A say.
Third minute: A compliments B and/or makes corrections.
Fourth minute: B speaks. Same topic, or a new one.
Fifth minute: A "plays back" what s/he heard B say.
Sixth minute: B compliments A and/or makes corrections.

Lead a culminating discussion. Ask the students these and other open-ended questions:
— *How did you feel when you listened like a tape recorder?*
— *How did you feel when you were the speaker, and were listened to well?*
— *How did you know you were listened to?*

Communication Is the Pilot

Practice in Precise Communication

Relates to:	Language Arts (oral language)
Objective(s):	The students will demonstrate the importance of precise communication in a simulated high-risk situation.
Time:	approximately 40 minutes
Materials needed:	numerous large objects, such as plants, furniture and/or trash cans
Directions:	**In an outdoor or large indoor area, set up an obstacle course using the plants, furniture, trash cans, etc.** This is the "runway" over which the "pilots" in this activity must be guided.

Talk with the students about how important it is for people to communicate clearly and accurately. Ask them to imagine what would happen if airplane pilots didn't communicate clearly with air traffic controllers, or quarterbacks didn't communicate accurately with their football teams. Airplanes would crash, and football teams wouldn't be able to run their plays.

Blindfold one student and spin him/her around at one end of the runway. This person is the pilot. Station a second student at the other end of the runway—the pilot's destination. Announce that this person is the air traffic controller. In your own words, explain: *When you are the air traffic controller, it is your job to guide the pilot (called "Captain") step-by-step through the obstacles using <u>words only</u>. If the pilot touches anything, it counts as a crash, and your turn is over. The pilot may direct questions to the air traffic controller. The rest of us will be very quiet during the exercise.*

Lead a summary discussion. After several students have had an opportunity to try the two roles, ask the students:
— *What can we learn from this experiment?*
— *What are some examples of other situations in which it would be essential to communicate very clearly?*

The Big Muddy

Group Experiment and Discussion

Relates to:	Language Arts (oral language)
Objective(s):	The students will: —demonstrate how communication can become distorted when a message is repeated again and again. —identify gossip and rumors as examples of oft-repeated and distorted messages.
Time:	approximately 10 to 20 minutes
Directions:	**Ask the students to sit down with you in a circle.** Then, in your own words, explain: *This may seem like a sharing circle, but it's not. This is an experiment called, "The Big Muddy." I'm going to whisper something into the ear of the person on my right, and try not to let the rest of you hear what I say. Then she will whisper it into the ear of the person on her right, and he will do the same, until everyone has heard the message and whispered it to the next person. After the last person has heard the message, he will say it out loud. Then I will tell you what I said in the beginning. Let's do it and see what happens.*

Begin the experiment: As the message is whispered, encourage the students to be as quiet as possible, and to observe each whisperer and listener in turn. Ask the last person who hears the message to repeat it out loud. Then tell the group what you said to the first person when you started the experiment. The difference between the two messages will probably cause amazement and laughter.

Suggest that the students do the activity again, and ask a volunteer to start a new message. As time allows, give everyone an opportunity to start a message.

Between experiments, facilitate discussion. Ask the students why they think the activity is called, "The Big Muddy." Talk about how communication can become muddy when it is passed from one person to another many times. Discuss the similarities between this experiment and gossip or rumors.

Dear Pen Pal...
Communicating Through Letter-Writing

Relates to: Language Arts (listening, writing, and reading)

Objective(s): The students will:
— write a series of letters to a pen pal.
— recognize letter-writing as an effective way to communicate with another person.

Time: approximately 15 to 20 minutes per letter-writing session.

Materials needed: a copy of Beverly Cleary's *Dear Mr. Henshaw* (1983) or Patricia MacLachlan's *Sarah, Plain and Tall* (1985), pencils and lined paper

Directions: **Preparation:** To acquire pen pals for your students, communicate with a teacher at another school who teaches the same grade level as you, and who will agree to a regular exchange of letters throughout the school year.

Before starting the project, read to your class a book in which letter-writing plays a significant role. *Dear Mr. Henshaw* and *Sarah, Plain and Tall* are two good choices. During and after your reading of the book, talk about how important it is for the characters to communicate by writing letters. Ask a few thinking questions like these:
— *Why do you think it was important for the characters to write letters?*
— *How does letter-writing help them understand themselves as well as others?*
— *What kinds of information do they share in their letters?*

Announce that the students that they are going to have an opportunity to meet new friends through letter-writing. These friends will be known as pen pals. Have the students write introductory letters. Explain: *Start your letter with the greeting, "Dear Pen Pal." Relate general information about yourself; for example, describe yourself and your family, your interests, hobbies, talents, school activities, and pets. If you like, you may enclose a drawing or photograph.*

Send the letters in a single envelope to the other classroom teacher. Request that s/he read the letters and match them to students with similar interests and/or writing abilities. From that point on, the students can use each other's names on the letters. Make an agreement with the other teacher to exchange letters on a regular basis throughout the year and to send all the letters at once. Try to ensure that every child sends and receives a letter at the same time as the rest of the class.

Invite the students to share their thoughts and feelings about the letters they receive. If a student wants to share his/her letter with the rest of the class, allow it. Such sharing can spark discussion concerning how to communicate better in writing.

Periodically assess the activity. Question the students to help them (and you) evaluate the experience:
— *What are your thoughts about the letter you just received from your pen pal?*
— *How do you feel about the letter you just wrote to your pen pal?*
— *Is there something you can do to make your letters more interesting?*
— *Are there suggestions you can make, or questions you can ask, to encourage your pen pal to write more interesting letters?*
— *Is there someone else who would be happy to receive a letter from you? Who?*

At the end of the school year, some of your students may elect to continue writing to their pen pals at home. That should indicate to you just how meaningful the letter-writing project has been.

Can You Tell How He or She Feels?

Pantomime and Discussion

Relates to: Drama and Language Arts (oral language)

Objective(s): The students will:
— demonstrate nonverbal behaviors appropriate to specific feelings.
— correctly identify feelings based on body language, facial expressions, and other nonverbal cues.

Time: approximately 30 minutes

Materials needed: descriptions of situations written on small pieces of paper, folded and placed in a container—one description for every two students. The descriptions should portray a variety of emotion-producing situations, like: "You just got a new puppy and your friend is very jealous." or "You and your friend are walking down a dark street at night. Suddenly, you hear a strange noise, but your friend doesn't hear it. S/he thinks you're making it up."

Directions: **Ask the students to pair up.** Have each pair draw one sheet of paper with a situation written on it. Direct each pair to go off to a private place for five minutes and plan a short pantomime of the situation. Explain that the students are to act only with their faces and bodies. They may neither say words, nor make vocal noises. The object is to do such a good job of acting that the class will be able to tell how each actor is <u>feeling</u> in his/her role. If the class can guess the situation, that's fine, but it is not necessary.

When the students have finished planning, have them enact their pantomimes one pair at a time. Enjoy each pantomime and applaud when it is over.

After each pantomime, ask the class to tell the actors how they appeared to be feeling in their roles. Finally, ask the actors to describe the situation they were acting out.

Lead a summary discussion. Ask the students:
— *Do our bodies and faces have a language of their own?*
— *What did you learn about that language through this activity?*

Not a Word Was Spoken, But I Knew How the Person Felt

A Sharing Circle

Relates to:	Language Arts (oral language)
Objective(s):	The students will identify feelings expressed by nonverbal clues in specific situations.
Directions:	**As necessary, review the sharing circle rules.**

Introduce the topic. In your own words, say to the students: *Our topic for today is, "Not a Word Was Spoken, But I Knew How the Person Felt." We tend to think we communicate with just the words we speak. However, we also give off clear messages <u>without</u> saying a word. Or we say words, but our bodies say something very different from our words. Think of a time when someone you know didn't say a word, yet you took one look and knew that person was unhappy or angry or delighted or scared. Describe how you think the person felt, and what it was about how the person looked that communicated his or her feelings so clearly. Take a few moments to think it over. The topic is, "Not a Word Was Spoken, But I Knew How the Person Felt."*

Involve the students. Invite them to take turns speaking. Listen carefully and encourage the other members of the circle to do the same. Thank each person who shares, and remember to take a turn yourself.

Summary questions:

—*How were you able to tell what the person was feeling without being told?*
—*What were the most obvious clues to the person's feelings?*
—*If you didn't know someone, do you think you could tell how that person was feeling? Why or why not?*

Speak Up, Speak Clearly!

Experience Sheet and Discussion

Relates to:	Language Arts (oral language)
Objective(s):	The students will: —demonstrate how unclear communication can lead to misunderstandings. —substitute clear for unclear communication in two dramatized situations.
Time:	approximately 30 minutes
Materials needed:	the experience sheets entitled, "Can You Say It Better?" (one per student)
Directions:	**Begin by talking with the students about how much people depend on their ability to communicate with each other.** Mention how communication is one of those things that can be very good or very bad. Bad communication causes misunderstandings and other problems. Bad communication can result from <u>unclear communication,</u> or <u>no communication at all</u>.
	Distribute the experience sheets. Ask the students to read the descriptions of the two situations with you.
	Have the students form groups of three to five. Tell them that they are going to act out the situations in the cartoons. Have half of the groups act out the first cartoon. Assign the second cartoon to the other half. Explain to the students: *I'd like each group to plan and rehearse <u>two</u> short skits. In the first skit, act out the situation the way it is written, showing how poor communication caused problems. In the second skit, have the characters communicate better, so that no problems occur. Each skit should be 1 to 3 minutes long.*
	Give the students 10 to 15 minutes to plan and rehearse their skits. Then ask them to perform for the total group. At the end of each small group's second skit, ask the students: —*What was the cause of the problem in the first skit?* —*Can you think of other things that could be done in the second skit to improve communication?* —*Do any of these situations remind you of times when you were involved in a misunderstanding? What happened?*

Can You Say It Better?

Here are two situations in which kids are not communicating well. Read each one. Then follow the directions—<u>and help them communicate better!</u>

Situation 1: Randy and Sue like each other, but both are a little shy. Sue just got a new haircut, and Randy thinks it's cute. When she looks at him, he says, "Hey, your hair is short and it's too neat!" He sticks his fingers in her hair and messes it up. The other kids laugh. Sue moves away quickly. She thinks to herself, "I guess Randy doesn't like my new haircut, and he doesn't seem to like me anymore either."

What <u>could</u> Randy say instead? What would Sue say to him? Fill in the bubbles.

Situation 2: Bill and Bud are pals. They decide to go on a five mile hike to the top of a big hill. They agree to meet at the one mile point. Bill says, "It's going to be great! I'll bring some stuff." Bud says, "Yeah, that's good. So will I." They meet at the right place at the right time, but each boy has a blanket and a snake bite kit. Neither has food or water, and they are already hungry and thirsty.

What <u>could</u> Bill and Bud say to each other to make a better plan? Fill in the bubbles.

DEVELOPING RESPECT FOR SELF AND OTHERS

The activities in this segment draw student attention to the fact that no two people are exactly alike. The point is gently made that, because each human being is unique, he or she is very special and valuable. Students are thus assisted to respect and esteem themselves and others as well.

Make Mine a Mixed Bouquet!

Art Activity

Relates to: | Art and Language Arts (listening and speaking)

Objective(s): | The students will:
—identify characteristics that make people different.
—describe the importance of celebrating differences among people.

Time: | approximately 40 minutes

Materials needed: | colored poster paper, magazines containing photos and illustrations of people and flowers (National Geographic would be excellent), scissors, glue, and magic markers in various colors; a bouquet containing several different kinds of flowers (optional)

Directions: | **Begin this activity by talking to the students about the enormous varieties of flowers that are available to grow, or to buy from the florist.** Point out that if they were to go to a florist, they could choose a bouquet made up of only one type of flower, or they could choose a mixed bouquet. Talk about the advantages of choosing a mixed bouquet. Mention that the variety of colors, shapes, textures, and scents would be beautiful, interesting, and stimulating to the senses. (If you brought a bouquet of flowers, use it as an example.)

Compare variety in flowers to variety in people. Point out that the different personalities, colors, backgrounds, religions, and talents in people are even more exciting.

Divide the students into groups of three or four, and distribute the materials. Tell the students that each group is going to make two mixed bouquets—one of flowers, and one of people. In your own words, explain: *Look through the magazines, and cut out pictures of different kinds of people, and different kinds of flowers. Find as much variety as you can. On one sheet of poster paper, arrange a collage of the people in the shape of a bouquet. On the other sheet of poster paper, do the same with the flowers. When you have finished your arrangements, glue the pictures down. Use the magic* *markers to draw a vase, and to attach a stem with leaves to each person or flower. Complete the collages by adding additional decorations with the magic markers.*

Circulate and talk with the students while they are creating. Ask them to guess where the people in their pictures work and live, and how they think the people would get along if they knew they were all part of the same bouquet. Talk about the richness that results from combining many unique individuals—whether they are people or flowers.

When the collages are done, put them up for all to see. Title the display, "Make Mine a Mixed Bouquet!"

Celebrating Our Differences

A Class Discussion

Relates to:	Language Arts (oral language)
Objective(s):	The students will: —identify ways in which people are different. —identify differences between themselves and another student. —describe benefits and problems that result from differences among people.
Time:	approximately 30 minutes
Materials needed:	chalkboard and chalk, or chart paper and magic marker
Directions:	**Discuss with the class the many ways in which people are different.** On chalk board or chart paper, write these terms: *race, religion, gender, handicap, ethnicity, economic level, place of residence, education, values.* **Define the terms, giving several examples of each.** Point out that these are some of the major ways in which people are different. Ask the students: —*How do people react to these differences in others?* —*What would the world be like if we were all the same?* —*How do you feel when you are with someone who is different from you?* —*If you feel uncomfortable around someone who is different from you, what can you do about it?* —*How do you feel when someone puts you down because <u>you</u> are different?* **Have the students pair up with the person next to them.** Tell them to turn toward each other, without leaving the large circle. Say: *Look at your partner. Notice as many things as you can about your partner that are different from you. Tell your partner one of the things you notice. Listen while s/he tells you how <u>you</u> are different. Then think about the ways in which you and your partner are the same, and take turns describing to your partner one of those similarities.* **Lead a summary discussion.** Ask the students these and other questions: —*How many things did you notice about your partner that were different? ...the same?* —*Do you normally notice those things? Why or why not?* —*What can you learn from people who are different from you?*

A Friend of Mine Who Is Different From Me

A Sharing Circle

Relates to:	Language Arts (oral language)
Objective(s):	The students will: —identify ways in which friends are unique and different. —state the importance of respecting differences among people.
Directions:	**Review the sharing circle rules.** Ask the students to name their favorite sharing circle rule and to describe why they like it best. Take your turn last, and name any rules that haven't been mentioned.
	Introduce the topic. In your own words, say to the students: *Today's topic is, "A Friend of Mine Who Is Different From Me." Think of a friend of yours who is different from you in some important way. Perhaps your friend is of a different race or religion, or is a lot older or younger than you. Maybe your friend would rather read a book while you watch television, or collect aluminum cans while you collect bugs. Do you have a friend who uses a wheelchair, or stutters, or goes to the hospital for dialysis treatments every few days? Don't mention your friend's name, but tell us how he or she is different from you, and what you particularly enjoy about this friendship. Let's think about it for a few moments. The topic is, "A Friend of Mine Who Is Different From Me."*
	Involve the students. Invite them to take turns speaking, and encourage them to listen carefully to one another. Don't allow negative interruptions, and be sure to take a turn yourself.
Summary questions:	—*When a person thinks or talks differently, or looks different, does that make him or her less worthy of respect? Why or why not?* —*What can we gain by having friends who are different from us?* —*What would happen if we insisted that all our friends be just like us?*

Try Out a Handicap

Experiment and Field Trip

Relates to:	Social Studies and Language Arts (oral language)
Objective(s):	The students will: —simulate a specific handicapping condition and experience it for two or more hours. —describe problems encountered while "handicapped." —describe the reactions of other people to the handicap.
Time:	two or more hours
Materials needed:	ear plugs, crutches, bandages or cloths to use as slings; surgical tape, pieces of lightweight wood or plastic to use as splints; and one or more wheelchairs, if you can obtain them; adult volunteers to accompany the students on the field trip portion of the activity
Directions:	**Tell the students that they are going to get a very small taste of what it's like to have a handicap.** They can be deaf, speech impaired (with mouth partially or completely taped), or "lose" an arm, leg, or both legs. Explain that while they are "handicapped," they will go out in public, and will have a chance to experience how other people react to them, and what sorts of adjustments they have to make in their normal behavior in order to participate in routine activities. **Have each student choose a partner, and pick a handicap.** If one member of a pair decides to experience a hearing loss by wearing ear plugs, the other should choose something different, like the "loss" of an arm. This way the students can compensate for each other's limitations, which will ensure that the experiment is a safe one. **Have the students splint, bandage, and otherwise prepare each other for the experiment.**

When everyone is ready, take a city bus ride. Pick a destination like a shopping mall, so that the students can move about and get the feel of their "handicaps," while experiencing other people's reactions to them. Tell the students to be alert to all aspects of the experience, so that they will be prepared to talk about it at the next class meeting.

At the next class session, use these and other questions to spark a discussion:
— *What kinds of things did you have to do to adjust to your handicap?*
— *How did other people treat you?*
— *What was it like getting on and off the bus? . . . going through doors? . . . going to the bathroom? . . . passing other people?*
— *What effect did this experience have on your attitudes toward people with handicaps?*

Happy Birthday to All!

Multicultural Research

Relates to:	Social Studies and Language Arts (reading, writing, oral language, and listening)
Objective(s):	The students will demonstrate an understanding of how different cultures celebrate birthdays.
Time:	approximately 30 minutes for library research, and 15 to 20 minutes for discussion
Materials needed:	books about different countries and library reference books; pencils, writing paper, and 12-inch by 18-inch drawing paper; crayons, colored markers, or colored pencils
Directions:	**Ask the students:** *What is your favorite celebration?* Many of them will answer: *My birthday.*

Lead a discussion about birthdays and why they make people feel so special. Ask the students how they celebrate birthdays in their families. Write "Birthday Activities" on the board, and list birthday cake, candles, "Happy Birthday" song, games, presents, and other ideas the children contribute. Talk briefly about these birthday traditions. Then explain that the students are going to have an opportunity work in small groups, conducting research to find out how birthdays are celebrated in other countries.

Divide the class into groups of 3 or 4 and assign each group a country. Explain that the groups are to look in the library for books about their country, and are to try to find out how birthdays are celebrated there. Show the students how to use the card catalogue. Demonstrate how to locate the name of the country or other descriptors, such as "birthdays," "customs," and "cultures." Urge the groups to take notes, and suggest that they draw pictures of the birthday customs and traditions they identify. Here are some examples of what they might find:

- **Mexico:** The birthday person is awakened early for good luck by a song from friends and/or family.
- **Israel:** Friends raise and lower the birthday child (in his/her chair) once for every year of age.

- **Russia:** A birthday pie is made and toothpicks are placed in the pie, spelling out "Happy Birthday."
- **Italy:** A birthday dinner is prepared and several tarts and cakes are served.

Invite each group to give a short oral presentation. Ask the groups to share any pictures they drew to illustrate the birthday customs. Display the drawings on a bulletin board, and ask the students to write captions for them.

Lead a summary discussion. Ask the students these and other open-ended questions:
— *How do you think birthday celebrations show respect for people?*
— *How would you like to celebrate your birthday?*
— *How can you help others have a special birthday?*

Extension: As a follow-up activity, let the students create *new* birthday customs. Ask them to write and illustrate descriptions of their newly created birthday celebrations.

Tasting Different Cultures

Reading, Discussion, and Experiencing

Relates to:	Social Studies and Language Arts (reading and speaking)
Objective(s):	The students will: —demonstrate respect for and understanding of differences among people, cultures, and lifestyles. —taste food representing different cultures and describe their reactions.
Time:	approximately 1 to 1 1/2 hours
Materials needed:	a copy of Tomie dePaola's *Watch Out for Chicken Feet in Your Soup* (New York, Simon & Schuster, 1974), a large wall map of the world, tagboard sentence strips, paper plates and napkins, and plastic utensils
Directions:	**Plan a cross-cultural food sampling day for the students.** Ask parents a week in advance if they will make simple ethnic foods that can be cut into bite-size pieces for the students to sample. Try to have a variety of cultures represented. Some examples might be lumpia (Philippines), guavas (Polynesian islands), scones and jam (England), roll tacos (Mexico), hummous and pita bread (Lebanon), or buñuelos (Columbia).
	Read the students dePaola's book *Watch Out for Chicken Feet in Your Soup.* It's about two young boys, Joey and Eugene, who go to visit Joey's Italian grandmother. She feeds them homemade chicken soup (complete with chicken feet) and spaghetti. She also invites Eugene to help her make bread dolls and sends the two boys off with their arms filled with freshly baked bread.
	Discuss the story. After reading the story, talk about the soup with chicken feet. Ask the students if anyone has ever had soup like that. Use this example as a springboard to a discussion on foods that are popular with different ethnic groups. If you have pictures of foreign foods, show them to the students and ask if anyone has tried them. Tell the students that some of their parents have brought foods representing different cultures, and that they are going to have an opportunity to taste them.

Taste the foods. As the students sample each dish, write the name of the food on a strip of tagboard and pin it on a large wall map of the world, indicating where that kind of food originated. As the students are sampling the foods, ask them why they think it is important to try foods from different cultures. Discuss how it helps people understand and appreciate those who are different from them.

Conclude the activity. Let each student choose one of the foods tasted and draw a picture of it. Then have that child write (or dictate) a sentence below the picture describing his/her experience tasting that food. Post the pictures on the bulletin board.

Extension: Experiment with additional activities that teach about other cultures, such as breaking a piñata, doing a Chinese dragon dance, or making Japanese fish kites.

Alternative: Another book that focuses on eating rituals in other cultures is *How My Parents Learned to Eat* by Ina Friedman, illustrated by Allan Say, Houghton Mifflin, 1984.

It's in the Bag!

Speaking/Collecting Activity

Relates to:	Language Arts (oral language)
Objective(s):	The students will select and describe symbols of things that are important to them.
Time:	approximately 30 minutes
Materials needed:	"Me" bags—one per student—containing things that represent the student's interests
Directions:	**Preparation:** One class session before this activity, ask the students to gather pictures, treasures, and memorabilia, place them in a brown paper bag, and bring the bag to the next class. Show them an example, by displaying a bag of your own memorabilia.

Have the students form a circle with their bags in front of them. Ask for volunteers, or draw names to determine the order of sharing.

Explain: *Pick items out of your bag, show them, and share with the class what each thing is and why it is important to you. Tell us if it is something you like or dislike, and how you came to have this thing. For example, you might explain that you brought ticket stubs from a special movie or concert you attended. Or you might show a picture of a ballerina because you want to take dance lessons and would like to be a performer someday.*

As the students share, some of them may need a little prompting from you. If they are shy or reluctant, ask questions like, *Was that a gift?* or *Would you like to tell us why that is important to you?* Make sure the students take their bags with them when they leave for the day.

Alternative: Have the students make collages out of magazine pictures that show likes and dislikes. Make a scrap book of special things.

Walk a Mile in My Moccasins
Experiment, Dyads, and Discussion

Relates to: Language Arts (oral language)

Objective(s): The students will:
— describe what it is like to walk in the shoes of another student.
— listen to and verbalize understanding of another student.

Time: approximately 20 minutes

Materials needed: an extra pair of socks for each child (optional)

Directions: **Have the students form a circle.** Explain that they are going to find out what it feels like to walk in someone else's shoes. Tell them to count off by two's. Ask the 2's to remove one shoe and place it in the center of the circle. Tell all of the students to close their eyes. While their eyes are closed, mix up the shoes. Then tell the 1's to reach in and take the first shoe they touch. Tell the students to open their eyes.

In your own words, explain: *Find the person whose shoe you have. Put on both of your partner's shoes, while he or she puts on your shoes. If you're not wearing socks, use one of the extra pairs I've provided. If you are wearing socks, but would like to wear an extra pair over your own, that's OK too. Now, take a short walk with your partner and talk about what it's like to wear each other's shoes. If the shoes are too small for you, notice what that feels like, and do the best you can.*

Allow the students to walk and talk for five to ten minutes.

Still wearing each other's shoes, have the partners sit together and take turns sharing in response to one of the following topics:
• A Time I Was Misunderstood
• I Was Treated Unfairly Because I'm Different

Tell the students that when it is their turn to listen, they are to be very attentive and do their best to understand their partner's experience. When their partner is finished speaking, they are to say very firmly and warmly, "I understand." Allow about two minutes of sharing per child.

Lead a summary discussion. Ask the entire class to answer these questions:
— *How did you feel when you were wearing your partner's shoes?*
— *Did you learn anything new about your partner?*
— *Why is it important to try to understand each other's experiences and differences?*

A Way I Show Respect for Others

A Sharing Circle

Relates to:	Language Arts (oral language)
Objective(s):	The students will describe specific behaviors that demonstrate respect for others.
Directions:	**As necessary, review the sharing circle rules.**
	Introduce the topic. In your own words, say to the students: *The topic for this circle is, "A Way I Show Respect for Others." There are many ways that we can show respect for other people. Tell us about a way that you frequently use. Maybe you remember to say please and thank you, or try never to interrupt others when they're talking, or hold doors when you go through them so they won't swing back and smack the people behind you. Perhaps you try not to say critical things about others, or maybe you listen respectfully to the opinions of people you disagree with. Tell us what you do that is respectful, and how you learned to do it. Think about it for a few moments. The topic is, "A Way I Show Respect for Others."*
	Involve the students. Invite each person to take a turn speaking, while everyone else listens carefully, without interrupting. Be sure to take a turn yourself.
Summary questions:	*— How do you feel about <u>yourself</u> when you show respect for others?* *— If <u>you</u> want to be respected, will showing respect for others help? How?* *— Should we show respect for people we don't like? Explain.*

How I Show Respect for Myself

Experience Sheet

Relates to:	Health and Language Arts (writing)
Objective(s):	The students will describe ways in which they show respect for themselves.
Time:	approximately 15 minutes
Materials needed:	the experience sheet entitled, "How I Show Respect for Myself"
Directions:	**Duplicate the experience sheet and give each student a copy.** Briefly review the directions. Make sure that the students understand the concept that self respect, and the lack of it, are readily demonstrated in behavior. That liking and respecting oneself are not just feelings, they are actions.

In each category, have the students write at least one thing they do to demonstrate respect for themselves and their bodies. When they are finished, allow the students to share what they have written with a partner or in small groups.

Lead a discussion. Ask the students these and other open-ended questions to stimulate further thinking:
— *What is respect?*
— *How is respecting yourself similar to respecting your parents, your flag, or your principal? How is it different?*
— *Which part of the experience sheet was hardest to complete? Why?*
— *What have you learned from this activity?*

Conclude the activity. Suggest that the students take their experience sheets home and share them with a parent or other caregiver.

How I Show Respect for Myself

Respecting yourself means that you think positively about yourself and treat yourself well. In each category below, write one or more activities that you do regularly to demonstrate that you respect yourself.

I respect my body:

Nutrition: _____

Exercise: _____

Hygiene: _____

Sleep: _____

Grooming: _____

I respect my mind:

Study habits: _____

New things I am learning: _____

What I am curious about: _____

I respect my feelings:

How I express my feelings: _____

How I reduce stress: _____

How I make myself feel happy: _____

I respect my behavior:

Good habits I have: _____

How I manage my time: _____

_____

BUILDING TRUSTING RELATIONSHIPS

Allowing oneself to trust another when trust is warranted, and becoming a trustworthy individual oneself, are important developmental milestones, thus the concepts of trust and trustworthiness form the conceptual basis for this segment. The activities assist students to realize that it is through trust and cooperation that the needs of people are generally met.

A Time I Had Fun with a Friend

A Sharing Circle

Relates to:	Language Arts (oral language)
Objective(s):	The students will... —describe enjoyable times spent with friends. —describe the value of leisure activities.
Directions:	**As necessary, review the sharing circle rules.** **Introduce the topic.** Say to the students: *We all have work to do, both at home and at school. Work is important. But fun and play are important too. Today we're going to talk about having fun. Our topic is, "A Time I Had Fun with a Friend."* *Think of something fun that you did with a friend. Maybe you and your friend went to a movie together—or to Disney World. Perhaps you played dress-up together, or hide-and-seek. Or maybe you went to your friend's house and played in the bedroom with his or her toys. Did you share an ice cream with your friend after school? Did you play a video or computer game together? Take a few minutes to think of something you did with a friend that you enjoyed. Raise your hand when you are ready to speak. Our topic is, "A Time I Had Fun with a Friend."* **Involve the students.** Invite the students to take turns sharing. Listen attentively to each person who speaks, and encourage the other students to do the same. Thank each one who shares. Remember to take a turn yourself. Let the students know that adults enjoy the leisure time that they spend with friends, too.
Summary questions:	—*What kinds of fun things do we do with our friends?* —*Do our friends have fun doing those things too?* —*How can you tell if a person is having fun?* —*Why is it important to do enjoyable things when we're not working?* —*What would it be like if we worked all the time and never had fun?*

Something I Like About One of My Best Friends

A Sharing Circle

Relates to:	Language Arts (oral language)
Objective(s):	The students will identify specific qualities they appreciate in their friends.
Directions:	**As necessary, review the sharing circle rules.**

Introduce the topic. In your own words, say to the students: *The topic for our circle today is, "Something I Like About One of My Best Friends." Most of us have several close friends, or "best" friends. Think about one of the things that you especially like about one of your best friends. Is it how he treats you? Could it be that she walks home from school with you everyday? Perhaps your friend is funny, or helps you with your spelling. Maybe he plays two-square with you at recess. Don't tell us your friend's name, just the special thing that you like about him or her. Let's take a minute to think quietly about it before we share. The topic is, "Something I Like About One of My Best Friends."*

Involve the students. Invite each person to take a turn speaking, while everyone else listens carefully. Be sure to take a turn yourself.

Summary questions:

— Were we able to think of one thing that we liked about a friend?
— How were these things alike or different?
— Why is it important to think about what we like in a friend?

Making and Keeping Friends

Role Playing and Discussion

Relates to:	Drama and Language Arts (oral language)
Objective(s):	The students will: —describe how all persons need to belong and be accepted by others. —demonstrate desirable skills for interacting with and relating to others. —demonstrate tolerance and flexibility in group situations. —demonstrate respect and understanding of differences among people's cultures, life styles, attitudes, and abilities.
Time:	approximately 30 minutes
Directions:	**Introduce the activity.** In your own words say to the students: *We all need to be treated in friendly ways. And one of the best ways to be treated well <u>ourselves</u> is to be a good friend to <u>others</u> and to treat <u>them</u> well. So let's talk about friendship today. Let's act out, and show one another, how friendship really works. To get started, let's make a list of some ways to make a friend—ways that work well. Then we'll make a list of ways to keep a friend.* Under the heading, "Making Friends," list at least three strategies that the students describe. Do the same under the heading, "Keeping Friends." As each strategy is mentioned, discuss how ineffective it would be to do the opposite. For example, if a student says that to make a friend you need to introduce yourself and ask what the person's name is, you might say: *Right. Who wants to be friends with someone who calls you, "What's-your-name?* **Demonstrate.** Suggest to the students: *I've got some ideas for situations we can act out using the strategies on our lists. When I describe a situation, if you have an idea which strategy will work, raise your hand. If I call on you, come up in front of the class and act it out. If you want some other actors to help, you may call on them. Let me go first to show you what I mean. The first situation is: <u>You are at a friend's birthday party. One of your friend's cousins, who is your age, is there too—but you've never seen him before. How do you make friends with the cousin?</u>*

Ask volunteers to play the friend who is having the birthday, two or three children at the party (who are having a good time), and your friend's cousin. Tell the volunteers what you would like them to say and do. Then, dramatize the scene, introducing yourself to the cousin and demonstrating friendly behavior toward him or her. For example, you might offer to share the last piece of pizza with him, or pour her some punch when you refill your own glass. Afterward, ask the students: *What do you think of what I did to make friends with this person? How did he or she seem to like what I did?*

Choose volunteers to dramatize several additional scenarios. Help each one select a strategy and choose the appropriate number of actors. Assist with planning, as necessary. At the end of each dramatization hold a brief discussion with the entire group.

Possible scenarios for the "Making Friends" dramatizations:

1. You are playing a game with some of your friends in your front yard. A new girl in the neighborhood walks up and stands nearby watching.

2. The teacher asks you and a boy in your class whom you don't know very well to take a box of books to the library. You believe this boy is much smarter than you are.

3. A family of a different race moves into a house on your street. The family includes two children about your age. One day the children come out of the house just as you walk by on your way to school.

Possible scenarios for the "Keeping Friends" dramatizations:

1. Your friend telephones you, but you just sat down to dinner with your family and it isn't a good time to talk.

2. Your friend had a fight with her big sister and is feeling terrible.

3. You are at the movies with a friend. Just before the movie starts, another friend comes over and sits beside you and says, "Hi." These two friends of yours don't know each other.

Something I Do to Keep a Friend

A Sharing Circle

Relates to:	Language Arts (oral language)
Objective(s):	The students will identify behaviors that promote friendship.
Directions:	**As necessary, review the sharing circle rules.**

Introduce the topic. In your own words, say to the students: *Our topic for today's session is, "Something I Do to Keep a Friend." We all have new friends and old friends. What is it that we do to keep a friend for a long time? Think about one of the things you do to make certain that someone will keep choosing you as his or her friend. Are you kind to him? Do you play tether ball with her after school? Do you invite him to ride his bike with you to the park on Saturdays? Maybe you help him or her practice the multiplication tables. Perhaps you share your ice cream with her when you buy one. Think quietly about it for a few moments before we start. The topic is, "Something I Do to Keep a Friend."*

Involve the students. Invite them to take turns speaking, and encourage them to listen to each other carefully. Remember to take a turn yourself.

Summary questions:

—*Were we all able to think of something that we do to keep a friend?*
—*How were these things alike and different?*
—*Why is it helpful for us to think of something that we do to keep a friend?*

We Decided To Do It This Way

Group Decision Making

Relates to:	Math and Language Arts (oral and written language)
Objective(s):	The students will make a group choice from among several alternatives.
Time:	approximately 20 minutes
Materials needed:	writing paper and pens or pencils
Directions:	**Have the students form groups of four or five and announce that each group has $100 in its treasury.** Working cooperatively, the groups must decide how best to use the money. Explain: *Pretend that your group has $100 to spend. Working individually, think of the very best way to use your group's money. Then, when I tell you to, explain your recommendation to the other members of your group. The group must then make <u>one choice</u> from among all of the suggestions. Write down the final decision of your group.*

Allow two or three minutes for individual thought, and then encourage the groups to start making their group choices. Ask each group to indicate when it has completed the task. Don't proceed until all groups are finished.

Ask each group to present its choice to the class. Acknowledge the group's efforts and ask some open-ended questions to generate discussion:
—*How well did your group work together?*
—*How did you go about making your group choice?*
—*What might have happened if the members of your group didn't get along?*

Extension: Combine the small groups, increase the treasury to $500 and challenge the students can make a class decision.

Friends Support Each Other

A Cooperative Game

Relates to: Physical Education and Language Arts (oral language)

Objective(s): The students will:
—provide physical support to one another in a group experiment.
—describe how providing mutual support is important in relationships.

Time: approximately 15 minutes

Materials needed: an outdoor space, free of glass, rocks, or holes; or an indoor space with mats or carpeting

Directions: **Brainstorm with the students ways in which friends give each other support.** Include suggestions such as, "encouraging friends to do their best in a ball game or race," "helping friends with chores or homework," and "sharing P.E. equipment." Also include "listening to friends when they have important things to say," "sharing feelings," and "consoling friends when they are upset." Discuss with the students how they feel when supported by *their* friends in these ways.

Tell the students that they are going to play a game in which they give each other physical support. It is a fun game in which friends may end up struggling, stumbling, and giggling, as well as supporting each other. They will start with one partner, and add another each time they accomplish their task. Say to them: *You will begin the game by sitting on the ground, back-to-back with your partner, knees bent and elbows linked. All you have to do is stand up together. With a little practice and cooperation, it will be pretty easy.*

After the partners have mastered standing up back-to-back, have some of them divide and join other partners to make groups of three. Give them the same task. Then try groups of four, five, and so on. A whole group stand-up can be achieved by having everyone sit close and stand up quickly, at exactly the same moment.

Expect a lot of giggling and falling over. Don't be concerned if the large group stand-up doesn't work. The fun is in the trying.

Lead a culminating discussion. After groups of various numbers have made several attempts to stand up, gather the students together and talk about how they felt when they were able to stand up together. Ask them:

— *How did it feel to support each other, and cooperate with one another?*

— *Which assignment was easiest? ...hardest? ...most fun?*

— *Why is it important for friends to support each other?*

— *How would you feel if a friend didn't support you in something?*

String Painting with a Partner

Art Activity

Relates to:	Art and Language Arts (oral language)
Objective(s):	The students will: — work cooperatively in pairs to produce paintings. — describe the importance of cooperation in completing a team task.
Time:	approximately 30 to 40 minutes
Materials needed:	white construction paper, one 2-foot piece of string per child, and tempera paint in several colors
Directions:	**Tell the students that they are going to participate in a cooperative art activity that is done in pairs.** Partners can make two paintings so that each child can take home one of them. Before the activity begins, have the students pair up. If there is an extra person, you can be his/her partner.

Place the materials on large workspaces. Have each pair decide on two colors for its string painting. Contrasting colors, such as red and blue, or a light and dark color, work best. Tell the students: *First, fold your drawing paper in half. Then reopen it. One of you will dip your string into a color of paint, holding onto one end of the string. Carefully place the painted string on one half of the paper, creating some kind of a design. Keep holding the dry end of the string, and let it stick out of the paper, while your partner folds the other half of the paper over the string. Your partner will then press lightly with his/her hands on the outside of the paper while you pull out the string. Open the paper. Next, your partner will repeat the process with his/her string, using another color of paint, and will make a design over yours while you press on the paper.*

The result will be a beautiful two-color butterfly, with one color underneath the other. Let each team make two paintings. Be sure to allow time for clean up.

As the students work, ask them how they feel about creating a piece of art as a team. Do they need to have some special talent to do this? Do they need to cooperate to accomplish the task? Is it fun? Have the partners share their paintings with the group.

Extension: See if the partners would like to "dance" their paintings. Have them notice how the two colors relate to each other on the paper. What shapes and directions do they take? Play some music and let the partners choreograph their string paintings.

Getting From Here to There

Creative Movement

Relates to:	Physical Education
Objective(s):	The students will: —create and perform original movements with a partner. —demonstrate cooperative problem-solving with a partner.
Time:	approximately 10 to 15 minutes
Materials needed:	cassette recorder and tapes of lively "traveling" music.
Directions:	This is an energizing activity that requires quick decisions and encourages students to use their bodies in creative ways. Do it on a large, empty floor or grassy area, and be prepared for lots of laughter, cheering, and enthusiasm.

Have the students find partners and line up at one end of the floorspace or grassy area. Tell them: *The object of the activity is to get from one side of this space to the other using a creative movement that no one else has used. You and your partner may either create a single, cooperative movement, or you may do the same movement. If you both do the same movement, you must mirror each other. You may roll, crawl, hop, skip, etc. It's okay to hold hands or link in some other way, but you don't have to.*

Point out that the students must watch carefully to see what all other pairs do, so that they don't repeat any movement. Pairs should be planning their traveling movements while they are waiting, because when they reach the head of the line, they must be ready to go as soon as the pair in front of them reaches the other side.

It is the responsibility of *everyone* to stop any pair that repeats a movement that has already been done, and send that pair to the back of the line.

Start the cassette recorder, and begin the activity. If you like, when everyone succeeds in getting to the other side, surprise the students by reversing directions and having them return to the original side—still without repeating any movements.

An Activity I Enjoy with Friends

A Sharing Circle

Relates to:	Language Arts (oral language)
Objective(s):	The students will identify leisure activities pursued with friends and describe why they are valuable.
Directions:	**Review the sharing circle rules.** Ask the students if they think the group has followed the rules reasonably well in recent circles. Agree or disagree, as appropriate. If you or any of the students mentions a rule that has not been followed, discuss it briefly and urge everyone to abide by it.
	Introduce the topic. In your own words, say to the students: *Today's topic is, "An Activity I Enjoy with Friends." We all enjoy doing things with our friends. What do you particularly like to do? Maybe you enjoy playing a sport or working on model planes or cars. Perhaps you like to go to the shopping mall with your friends, or watch television. Do you and your friends play video games, or go bicycling or skating? Do you build things out of odds and ends, LEGOS, building blocks, or logs? Do you make up plays and act in them? Whatever it is you most enjoy doing with your friends, please tell us about it. I'll give you a few moments to decide. When you are ready, raise your hand. The topic is, "An Activity I Enjoy Doing with Friends."*
	Involve the students. Ask if anyone would like to share. If no one is ready, take your turn first. Listen attentively to the person who is speaking, and encourage the students to do the same. Individually thank each person who shares.
Summary questions:	—*What kinds of things did most of us enjoy doing with our friends?* —*Why do we often do different things with different friends?* —*Who usually decides what you and your friends are going to do? What do you do when you disagree?*

Building Friendship Through Trust
Story and Dramatization

Relates to:	Social Studies and Language Arts (oral language and listening)
Objective(s):	The students will: —act out a fable in which trust is built by caring actions. —demonstrate that trust is an important element in building friendship.
Time:	approximately 30 to 45 minutes
Materials needed:	a copy of the book *Androcles and the Lion* (adapted and illustrated by Janet Stevens, 1989); "found" materials to use as props
Directions:	**Read (or tell) the story of *Androcles and the Lion*.** It is an Aesop fable in which Androcles, a runaway slave in ancient Rome, encounters a lion with a large thorn stuck in its paw. He gently pulls the thorn out, much to the relief of the lion. Soldiers capture Androcles and send him back to Rome to stand trial. Another group of soldiers catches the lion and carries him back to Rome also. In those days runaway slaves were punished by being put into a large arena with hungry lions that attacked and ate them. Androcles is sent into the arena at the same time as a hungry lion. However, the lion doesn't attack him; it is the same lion he helped. Androcles and the lion are set free. Androcles is saved because of the trust he built with the lion through his caring actions. **After reading the story, review with the class the sequence of events.** List the characters on the board: Androcles, the lion, the cruel master, the soldiers, judges, and crowd at the arena. Discuss what actions each character takes in the story. Announce that the students are going to have a chance to act out the story. Ask volunteers to "become" the characters and guide them through a dramatization of *Androcles and the Lion*. Push back the desks, and use props from around the room. Enact the story several times so that every child has an opportunity to participate in at least one interpretation.

Lead a discussion. When everyone has had an opportunity to act in one dramatization, gather the students together and ask these and other open-ended questions to summarize the story's main concepts:

— *How was trust built between Androcles and the Lion?*
— *What are some caring things that people can do to build trusting relationships?*
— *Why is it important for friends to trust each other?*

Conclude the Activity. Ask the students if they can remember a caring action that someone took to win their trust. Give individuals an opportunity to share their experience with the class.

Someone Whose Friendship I Value

A Sharing Circle

Relates to:	Language Arts (oral language)
Objective(s):	The students will describe qualities that they value in a specific friendship.
Directions:	**Review the sharing circle rules.** After the students form a circle, ask them to take turns naming the ground rules. Fill in any that they forget.
	Introduce the topic. In your own words, say to the students: *Our topic today is, "Someone Whose Friendship I Value." When something is valuable to us, that usually means that it is worth a lot, and that it would be hard to replace. We value things, like bikes, casette players, and clothing. But we also value people. Think of someone whose friendship you value. Friendship with this person is worth so much to you that it would be hard to replace. Your friend could be someone you see at school, or someone who lives in your neighborhood. He or she could be an older person who takes you special places. Perhaps your friend is someone who teaches you a sport or other skill. Your friend might be a relative, like a brother or sister. It could even be a pet. Tell us who your friend is and what kinds of things you do with your friend. Think about it for a few moments. The topic is, "Someone Whose Friendship I Value."*
	Involve the students. Invite them to take turns sharing. Listen carefully to each person who contributes, and encourage the other students to do the same. Don't allow negative interruptions. Be sure to take a turn yourself.
Summary questions:	*—How do we know when we value something or someone?* *—What kinds of things make a friendship valuable?* *—Why is it important to know what we value?*

My Circle of Friends

1. Write the names of your friends on the lines provided around this "Circle of Friends."

2. Use magic markers or colored pencils to draw <u>yourself</u> on the figure without a face. Add <u>your</u> name to that line.

3. Draw a circle around each word that describes a good friend. Then draw a line connecting each circled word with a friend that the word describes. It's OK to connect the same word to more than one friend. You will probably end up with lines criss-crossing each other all over the circle!

IMPORTANT: This sheet is private. Take it home and fill it out. Keep it for yourself, so that you can think about your friends and what their friendship means to you. You don't have to show it to anyone, if you don't want to.

MANAGING CONFLICT

Interpersonal conflict is an inevitable part of life and cannot be entirely avoided, nor should it be in some cases. Therefore, the ability to *manage* conflicts is an important life skill. The activities in this segment assist students to understand the dynamics of conflict and to manage conflicts without jeopardizing self-esteem.

Conflict and Resolution

Learning Through Literature

Relates to:	Social Studies and Language Arts (reading, writing, listening, and oral language)
Objective(s):	The students will identify conflict situations between character elements in literature and describe how they are managed.
Time:	approximately 30 minutes of class time following completion of individual reading assignments
Materials needed:	Selected middle reading books in which conflicts between character elements can be easily identified (one title per child). Myths, fables, and folktales are good sources. Many children's novels also represent various types of conflict. Here are several suggested titles:

Armstrong, William, *Sounder* (racial prejudice, poverty, father in prison)

Blume, Judy, *Are You There God? It's Me, Margaret* (growing up, religious conflict)

Brechenfeld, Vivian, *Two Worlds of Noriko* (Japanese-American experience)

Byars, Betsy, *Summer of the Swans* (retarded brother)

Cleary, Beverly, *Dear Mr. Henshaw* (parents' divorce, loneliness)

Coerr, Eleanor, *A Thousand Paper Cranes* (death, cancer, family crisis)

Cohen, Barbara, *Molly's Pilgrim* (racial prejudice, new immigrant)

George, Jean Craighead, *My Side of the Mountain* (conflict with nature)

Juster, Norton, *The Phantom Tollbooth* (conflict with academic learning)

Lowry, Lisa, *Anastasia* series (growing up)

Paterson, Katherine, *The Great Gilly Hopkins* (abandonment, foster parents)

Paterson, Katherine, *Bridge to Terabithia* (friendship, death)

Sneve, Virginia, *When Thunder Spoke* (Indian boy's conflict with old culture)

Directions:

Tell the students you would like each of them to select and read a book in which the character elements are involved in one or more conflicts. Explain that one way to learn to manage conflict is to emulate characters in literature. Suggest the above titles or others that you or a children's librarian recommend. Help each student choose a book that is appropriate to his/her reading ability. Allow sufficient time for reading.

Explain to the students that a story plot involves conflict between character elements. Character elements include the actual characters, the environmental setting, and personality elements within a single character. Ask the students to think about the character elements in their books and the conflicts between them. Tell them that by making a chart (semantic map) of the character elements and conflicts, they will find it easier to see how conflict is managed (dealt with, not necessarily resolved) in the story.

Make a chart on the chalkboard. Draw a vertical line to form two columns. Write the heading "Character Element" at the top of column one and "Conflict" at the top of column two. Use a familiar fable, such as "The Lion and the Mouse" as an example. List the character elements and the conflicts as follows:

"The Lion and the Mouse"

Character Elements	Conflicts
• Lion and Mouse	• Mouse bothers lion by running across face.
	• Lion threatens to kill mouse.
• Personality of lion	• Lion shows feelings of superiority by laughing when mouse says he will someday repay the lion for sparing his life.
• Lion and environment	• Lion caught in hunter's net.

Discuss the elements and conflicts, and ask volunteers to tell how the conflicts are resolved or managed. For example, the conflict of the mouse bothering the lion is managed by the lion grabbing the mouse in his paw. The conflict of the lion's threat to the mouse is resolved by the mouse begging for mercy and promising to repay the lion's kindness some day. The conflicts of the lion and his environment as well as the lion's feelings of superiority are both resolved when the mouse saves the lion's life by chewing the ropes of the hunter's net, setting the lion free.

Have the students write the title of their book at the top of a piece of lined paper. Ask them to make two columns with headings like those on the board. Then invite them to list the character elements in the stories they read and the conflicts between those character elements. Remind the students that there will probably be conflicts between the main character and several other characters, and that each must be listed as a separate story element. Assist individual students, as necessary.

Ask individual volunteers to share their analyses with the class, explaining how various conflicts in their story are managed.

Lead a summary discussion. Ask the children some thinking questions such as the following:
— *What did you learn about conflict management from this activity?*
— *How can we apply what we learn from books to our own lives?*

Everybody's Got a Point of View
Listening, Writing, and Discussion

Relates to:	Language Arts (literature, writing, and oral language)
Objective(s):	The students will: —identify perception as a key element in conflict situations. —describe how the perceptions of people can differ. —describe ways of resolving conflict.
Time:	approximately 15 to 20 minutes
Materials needed:	a copy of "The Maligned Wolf" (provided)
Directions:	**Introduce the activity.** Call the class together and tell the students that you have a story to read to them, called "The Maligned Wolf."
	Begin reading the story. Very quickly, the students will recognize the story as *Little Red Riding Hood*, told from the point of view of the wolf. Expect excitement and keen interest at this point.
	Lead a discussion. Here are some questions to ask the students after you have finished reading the story: —*Have you heard this story before? What was different about this version?* —*Had you ever thought about how the wolf felt, or considered his point of view?* —*Why does everyone have a right to his or her own point of view?* —*What does hearing this story in this new way teach us?* —*What does this story teach us about conflicts?* —*What are some other stories that can be retold from the point of view of the villain? What about <u>Jack and the Beanstalk</u>? What would the giant say if we considered the story from his point of view?*
	Conclude the activity. Point out that the next time the children are about to get into a conflict with someone, they can help prevent or manage the conflict by considering things from the point of view of the other person and trying to get the other person to consider things from their point of view. Thank the children for listening and participating.

The Maligned Wolf

By Leif Fearn

The forest was my home. I lived there and I cared about it. I tried to keep it neat and clean.

Then one sunny day, while I was cleaning up some garbage a camper had left behind, I heard footsteps. I leaped behind a tree and saw a rather plain little girl coming down the trail carrying a basket. I was suspicious of this little girl right away because she was dressed funny—all in red, and her head covered up so it seemed like she didn't want people to know who she was. Naturally, I stopped to check her out. I asked who she was, where she was going, where she had come from, and all that.

She gave me a song and dance about going to her grandmother's house with a basket of lunch. She appeared to be a basically honest person, but she was in my forest and she certainly looked suspicious with that strange getup of hers. So I decided to teach her just how serious it is to prance through the forest unannounced and dressed funny.

I let her go on her way, but I ran ahead to her grandmother's house. When I saw that nice old woman, I explained my problem and she agreed that her granddaughter needed to learn a lesson, all right. The old woman agreed to stay out of sight until I called her. Actually, she hid under the bed.

When the girl arrived, I invited her into the bedroom where I was in the bed, dressed like the grandmother. The girl came in all rosy-cheeked and said something nasty about my big ears. I've been insulted before so I made the best of it by suggesting that my big ears would help me to hear better. Now, what I meant was that I liked her and wanted to pay close attention to what she was saying. But she makes another insulting crack about my bulging eyes. Now you can see how I was beginning to feel about this girl who put on such a nice front, but was apparently a very nasty person. Still, I've made it a policy to try to ignore put-downs, so I told her that my big eyes helped me to see her better.

Her next insult really got to me. I've got this problem with having big teeth. And that little girl made an insulting crack about them. I know that I should have had better control, but I leaped up from that bed and growled that my teeth would help me to eat her better.

Now let's face it—no wolf has ever eaten a little girl—everyone knows that. But that crazy girl started running around the house screaming with me chasing her trying to calm her down. I'd taken off the grandmother clothes, but that only seemed to make things worse.

All of a sudden the door came crashing open and a big lumberjack was standing here with his axe. I looked at him and all of a sudden it became clear that I was in deep trouble. There was an open window behind me and out I went.

I'd like to say that was the end of it. But that grandmother character never did tell my side of the story. Before long the word got around that I was a terrible, mean guy. Everybody started shooting at me. I don't know about that little girl with the funny red outfit, but *I* didn't live happily ever after. In fact, now us wolves are an endangered specie. And I'm sure that little girl's story has had a lot to do with it!

I Observed a Conflict

A Sharing Circle

Relates to:	Language Arts (oral language)
Objective(s):	The students will: —describe a conflict that they observed. —describe ways of dealing with reactions of others in conflict situations. —describe healthful ways of coping with conflicts, stress, and emotions.
Directions:	**Review the sharing circle rules.** Ask the students to state the rules that they remember. Add any that they fail to mention. Before beginning, elicit a commitment on the part of the students to follow the rules throughout the circle. **State the topic.** In your own words, say to the students: *Conflicts are normal events that occur between people, but they can sometimes be very troubling and hurtful. At other times, conflicts can lead to better understanding between people. We need to learn how to manage conflicts so that, when they occur, we can steer them in the direction of positive outcomes. Our topic today will help us begin thinking and talking about the subject of conflict. It is, "I Observed a Conflict."* *Can you think of a time, either recently or some time back, when you saw two people have an argument, a disagreement, or a fight? See if you can remember what caused it, and how each of the people seemed to feel. How did they act? How did you feel as the argument or fight was going on? We want to hear about the conflict, but please don't tell us who the people were, okay? Take a few moments to think about it. When you are ready, raise your hand. The topic is, "I Observed a Conflict."* **Involve the children.** Ask who would like to go first. If none of the students is ready, take your turn; then invite them again. As the students speak, model good listening by giving them your full attention.
Summary questions:	*—What caused the conflicts we described in this sharing circle?* *—How did people get hurt by the conflicts we described?* *—Did some of the conflicts work out OK?* *—Why is it impossible to go through life without ever getting into a conflict?*

I Almost Got Into a Fight

A Sharing Circle

Relates to: Language Arts (oral language)

Objective(s): The students will describe methods they used to prevent conflict situations from becoming fights.

Directions: **As necessary, review the sharing circle rules.**

Introduce the topic. In your own words, say to the students: *Our topic for this session is, "I Almost Got Into a Fight!" From time to time each of us has a disagreement or conflict with another person. Sometimes conflicts aren't very serious, and sometimes they are. Can you think of a time when something happened between you and someone else that almost caused you to get into a fight? Maybe you wanted to fight because you were upset. Or maybe the other person tried to start the fight. Perhaps you both felt like fighting, but then, somehow, you settled the problem peacefully. Tell us how the incident happened, and how you felt, but please don't tell us who the other person was. The topic is, "I Almost Got Into a Fight."*

Involve the students. Invite them to take turns sharing. Listen carefully to each one and guide the other students to do the same. Don't allow negative interruptions. Be sure to take a turn yourself.

Summary questions:
—*Is conflict always bad, or can it sometimes lead to good things?*
—*What were the main ways we kept these disagreements or conflicts from becoming big fights?*
—*Is fighting a good way to resolve conflict? Why or why not?*

Conflict Management Strategies

Experience Sheet, Drama, and Discussion

Relates to: Language Arts (reading and oral language) and Drama

Objective(s): The students will:
—demonstrate strategies for resolving conflicts with others.
—describe and discuss causes of conflict.
—demonstrate ways of dealing with reactions of others in conflict situations.

Time: approximately 10 to 15 minutes to read and discuss each conflict management strategy (may be done in several sessions)

Materials needed: a pencil and one copy of the experience sheet, "Conflict Management Strategies" for each student

Directions: **Distribute the experience sheets.** Write the words *conflict management* on the chalkboard. Define both words separately; then define the term. Ask:
— *How many of you have ever been in a conflict that was really terrible, where you or someone else got hurt physically, or had your feelings hurt badly?*
— *Have you ever been in a conflict that worked out well for everyone?*

Ask a few of the students who respond affirmatively to the second question to describe those conflicts. Then analyze them briefly. Point out instances in which the people involved used strategies or behaviors similar to those described in the experience sheet. Emphasize that by using these strategies, they showed respect for each other—and for themselves.

Read each strategy aloud to the students while they read along silently. Write the strategy on the chalkboard and define it. Discuss the strategy with the students—then give them opportunities to practice it. Here are some suggestions:
• **Active listening:** Ask volunteers to practice making statements (those listed on the experience sheet and others) that indicate they are listening.

- **"I" messages:** Think of several conflict situations and ask volunteers to role play them. Help the actors formulate first "you" messages (blaming, name-calling) and then "I" messages (stating feelings, perceptions). Discuss the differences.
- **Compromise:** Brainstorm a list of compromise statements like those listed in the experience sheet. Practice saying some of them.
- **Taking turns:** Describe a familiar conflict situation to the children, e.g., *two students want to use the class computer at the same time.* Allow volunteers to demonstrate different ways of "taking turns," such as flipping a coin, drawing straws, and choosing a number between one and ten.
- **Putting it off:** Let several students practice making statements that suggest putting off the resolution of the conflict until a later time. Discuss the importance of keeping the commitment to return to the conflict, rather than just forgetting about it.
- **Getting help:** Ask the students to remember times when they used this strategy. Discuss one or two examples.
- **Expressing regret:** The difference between apologizing and expressing regret is subtle even for adults, so spend some time discussing this one. Then let the students practice making the statements shown on the experience sheet.

Discuss unacceptable and "last resort" responses to conflict. List the words *violence*, *tattling*, and *running away* on the chalkboard. Discuss each one. Here are some suggestions for things you might say:

Violence: If someone becomes violent with you, you must either leave the situation or defend yourself. However, violence usually destroys any possibility of settling the conflict so that both people are satisfied. By the way, saying cruel things to another person is a form of violence.

Tattling: When you tell on someone, it is usually because you want to get the person in trouble. Tattling never helps settle conflicts; it only makes the other person mad. So, instead of tattling, manage your own conflicts. If you decide to ask for help, remember that the help is for <u>both</u> you and the other person in the conflict.

Running away: If you are about to get hurt, leave the situation as fast as you can. But don't get in the habit of running away from conflict. Respect yourself and the other person enough to stay and try to settle the conflict. Say how you feel and what you think. Listen. Use the conflict management strategies.

Conflict Management Strategies

Have you ever been in a conflict? Of course!
Some conflicts are terrible experiences that cause hurt feelings and even hurt bodies. Other conflicts aren't so bad. Some can even lead to good things. How does that happen? How can you make a conflict turn out well? By *managing* the conflict. Here are some ways to do it:

Listen—*actively!*
Often people get into conflicts because they don't really listen to each other or they misunderstand what they hear. So try *really* listening to the other person's point of view. Tune in to the words—and the feelings too. To let the other person know that you are listening, say things like:

"Okay, I'm listening."

"Go ahead. You talk first and I'll listen."

"Let me see if I heard you right. You said..."

Use "I" messages.
Show the other person that you are willing to take responsibility for your feelings and the way you view the conflict. Don't use name-calling, blaming "you" messages, like:

"Hey stupid, you hogged all the milk again!"

Instead, say what you think and how you feel, with an "I" message, like:

"I'm thirsty. I feel bad when there's no milk left for me."

Try to compromise.
If you are willing to give up a little of what you want, and the other person is too, then you can both have at least *part* of what you want. That's a *compromise*. You compromise when you make suggestions like these:

"I'll take half and you take half."

"I'll go to the park with you in the morning, if you'll go to the mall with me in the afternoon."

"I'll mow the lawn, and you sweep the walks."

Take turns.

Some conflicts happen because two people want the same thing at the same time. Show the other person that you are willing to be *second* sometimes. Flip a coin, draw straws, guess a number between one and ten, or say:

"You go first because I'm bigger."

Put it off.

If you are mad, tired, hungry, or in a hurry—or if you think the other person is—wait! Put off dealing with the conflict until later. Say:

"I want to settle this, but now's not the time. What about waiting until after lunch?"

"Everything seems to be going wrong. I'm too tired to think straight. Could we get back to this later?"

Get help.

Bring someone into the conflict who can help settle it. This may sound like tattling, but it's not. Tattling is trying to get the other person in trouble; getting help is asking another person to help straighten things out. For example, if you and a friend disagree about how a word should be pronounced, ask your teacher.

Express regret.

Let the other person know that you are sorry the conflict happened. You *don't* have to admit you are wrong or that the conflict is your fault. Just say:

"It's too bad this happened."

"I know you're upset and I feel bad about it."

Conflict Management Strategies on Stage

Drama and Discussion

Relates to:	Drama and Language Arts (oral language)
Objective(s):	The students will: —demonstrate five conflict management strategies. —discuss how each strategy works to reduce or resolve conflict.
Time:	approximately 30 to 40 minutes
Materials needed:	a chart showing the following conflict management strategies: *1) Sharing, 2) Listening, 3) Expressing Regret, 4) Putting Off, and 5) Compromising/Negotiating;* the following conflict management scenarios, each written on a separate piece of paper:

• Two people are arguing because they both want something. They agree to share the thing they both want. (Strategy: sharing.)

• Person A is mad at person B. Person A calms down after B listens to A respectfully. (Strategy: listening.)

• Person A is upset about something. Person B expresses understanding of A's feelings and tells A that s/he is sorry that A feels so bad. (Strategy: expressing regret.)

• Two people are already feeling irritable when they start to argue about something. They agree not to say any more now, and to settle the problem later, when they both feel better. (Strategy: putting off.)

• and B want to have different things, but they can only have one thing at a time. They agree to have some of what A wants first; then to have some of what B wants. (Strategies: compromising/negotiating.)

Directions:

Give the five pieces of paper with the conflict management scenarios written on them to five students, and ask each to choose a partner. Explain that each pair is to act out its conflict situation, and to demonstrate the management strategy listed.

Give the students five to ten minutes to prepare their skits. Provide assistance, as needed.

Invite the actors to perform their skits. After each skit, ask the audience which strategy was demonstrated, and put a check mark beside it on the chart. Hold a brief discussion regarding each strategy and how well it works in managing conflict.

I Got Into a Conflict

A Sharing Circle

Relates to:	Language Arts (oral language)
Objective(s):	The students will: —describe conflicts they have experienced and what caused them. —describe ways of dealing with the reactions of others in conflict situations. —identify strategies for resolving conflicts with peers and adults.
Directions:	**As necessary, review the sharing circle rules.**

Introduce the topic: Say to the students: *Our topic today is, "I Got Into a Conflict." Conflicts are very common. They occur because of big and little things that happen in our lives. And sometimes the littlest things that happen can lead to the biggest conflicts. This is your opportunity to talk about a time when you had an argument or fight with someone. Maybe you and a friend argued over something that one of you said that the other didn't like. Or maybe you argued with a brother or sister over what TV show to watch, or who should do a particular chore around the house. Have you ever had a fight because someone broke a promise or couldn't keep a secret? If you feel comfortable telling us what happened, we'd like to hear it. Describe what the other person did and said, and what you did and said. Tell us how you felt and how the other person seemed to feel. There's just one thing you shouldn't tell us and that's the name of the other person, OK? Take a few moments to think about it. When you are ready, raise your hand. The topic is, "I Got Into a Conflict."*

Involve the students. Ask if anyone is ready to share. If no one volunteers, take your turn first. Then invite the students again. Model good listening by giving each person your full attention. Thank the students for their contributions.

Summary questions:
—*How did most of us feel when we were part of a conflict?*
—*What kinds of things led to the conflicts that we shared?*
—*How could some of our conflicts have been prevented?*
—*What conflict management strategies could have been used in the situations that we shared? Be specific.*

Demonstrating Conflict Management Strategies

Role Play and Discussion

Relates to:	Drama and Language Arts (oral language)
Objective(s):	The children will: —describe how one's behavior influences the feelings and actions of others. —demonstrate skills in resolving conflicts with peers and adults. —describe and discuss causes of stress and conflict. —identify and select behaviors appropriate to specific emotional situations. —demonstrate ways of dealing with reactions of others under stress and conflict. —demonstrate healthful ways of coping with conflicts, stress, and emotions. **Note:** In this activity the children dramatize events disclosed in the sharing circle, "I Got Into a Conflict," and apply techniques presented in the experience sheet, "Conflict Management Strategies." Both are prerequisite activities.
Time:	approximately 40 minutes
Materials needed:	a list of the conflict situations discussed in the sharing circle, "I Got Into a Conflict;" a list of the conflict management strategies on chart paper, or a copy of the experience sheet, "Conflict Management Strategies" for each child
Directions:	**Introduce the activity.** In your own words suggest to the children: *In the sharing circle, "I Got Into a Conflict," we told one another about times we got into conflicts. Now let's act out some of the episodes we shared. If your episode is chosen, you will be the director. You can ask other "actors" to help you. Tell them what to say and do to make the event exactly like it was when it actually happened. Afterwards, the rest of us will suggest conflict management strategies that you can use to make the situation better. Pick one strategy and act out the situation again, using that strategy. The person who suggested the strategy will be your director for the second role play.*

Begin the dramatizations. Select a child whose conflict situation will lend itself well to role playing, and ask the child to direct and "star" in his or her own scenario. Assist with the selection and coaching of supporting actors. Then watch with the other children as the conflict scenario is recreated. Afterwards, ask the group: *Which conflict management strategies could be used in this scenario? Which strategies might help settle this argument (fight)?*

Call on several children and hear their ideas. Jot down all ideas on the chalkboard or chart paper. Then ask the "star" to choose one strategy and act it out, with the child who made the suggestion serving as the new director.

Debrief each scenario. Immediately after each set of dramatizations, ask these and other questions to help the children evaluate the results of their use of conflict management strategies:
— *How did you (the actors) feel, using the conflict management strategy?*
— *How do you (the actors) think it worked?*
— *How does the group think it worked?*
— *How many of you will try using this conflict management strategy to settle a real conflict?*

Select a second conflict situation and repeat the process. Continue with the dramatizations as long as the children remain interested.

Conduct a summary discussion. Give all of the children an opportunity to respond to this summarizing question:
— *What is the most important thing you have learned about conflict from this activity and the other conflict-management activities we have done?*

Conclude the activity. Thank the children for the fine acting, thinking, speaking and listening they demonstrated during this activity.

"I" Messages Ease Tense Situations
Drama and Discussion

Relates to:	Drama and Language Arts (oral language)
Objective(s):	The students will: —contrast the use of aggressive and assertive statements in hypothetical conflict situations. —describe how "I" messages ease conflict situations and help people take responsibility for their actions.
Time:	approximately 45 minutes
Materials needed:	the experience sheets entitled, *Don't Say "You," Say "I"* (one per student)
Directions:	**Begin by telling the students about two different ways that a person can respond to tense situations.** A person can say, "You . . .," or a person can say "I . . ." When you start a sentence with the word, *you*, it's a "you" message. When you start a sentence with the word *I*, it's an "I" message. "You" messages often lead to blaming and name calling. For example: *You did it, you dope!* "I" messages are usually more tactful. For example: *I didn't mean to hurt you. I regret what happened.*

Distribute the experience sheets. Tell the students to fill in the speech bubbles on their own, at some other time. Ask them to read the descriptions of the two situations with you. Choose four volunteers to play the parts of the individuals in the two cartoons (two per cartoon).

Explain: *Plan two short skits. In the first skit, the person who is <u>responding</u> to the situation should get upset and deliver a "you" message to the person who spoke first. Then the two of you should keep up the negative interaction for a while. In the second skit, the person responding to the situation should try to lighten things up by using an "I" message. We'll see how these two different ways of responding affect the people involved.*

Give the students ten to fifteen minutes to plan and rehearse their skits. Then ask them to perform for the total class. At the end of <u>each</u> small group's second skit, ask the students:

— *What were the effects of the "you" messages that were delivered in these skits?*

— *What were the effects of the "I" messages that were delivered in these skits?*

— *How can you remember to use "I" messages in conflict situations you face in your own life?*

Don't Say "You," Say "I"

Here are two tense situations. In each one, an "I" message could be used to lighten things up. Read each situation. Draw a picture of yourself in the cartoon. Then, using an "I" message, write your response to what the other person is saying.

Situation One: You are walking down the hall. You see the biggest bullies in the school slam your friend up against a wall. Then you hear them call your friend names. You feel terrible and would like to help, but just then your friend looks at you and angrily says . . .

Situation Two: You borrow your older sister's cassette recorder and a couple of tapes, but then the recorder stops running. You know you haven't done anything harmful to it, but when you give it back, she is very upset. She blames you by saying . . .

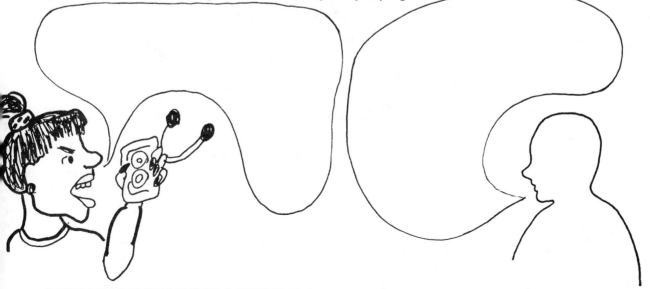

How I Used an "I" Message
A Sharing Circle

Relates to:	Language Arts (oral language)
Objective(s):	The students will: —describe specific incidents in which they used "I" messages. —state the benefits of using "I" messages in tense or conflict situations.
Note:	This circle should not be done until you have led the activity, "'I' Messages Ease Tense Situations."
Directions:	**As necessary, review the sharing circle rules.**
	Introduce the topic. In your own words, say to the students: *Our topic for this session is, "How I Used an 'I' Message." At our last meeting we did some skits involving "I" messages and "you" messages. Our experience sheets also covered "I" and "you" messages. Do you remember the differences between these two types of messages, and how they affect tense situations?* (Discuss, as necessary.) *In this sharing circle, we will each have a chance to tell about a time when we tried using an "I" message, and what happened when we did. If you haven't had a chance to use an "I" message yet, tell us about a time when you didn't use one, and how you think things would have turned out if you had. Tell us all about the incident, but don't tell us the names of the other people involved. Our topic is, "How I Used an 'I' Message."*
	Involve the students. Invite them to take turns speaking. Listen carefully to each one and guide the other students to do the same. Don't allow negative interruptions. Be sure to take a turn yourself.
Summary questions:	—*How did our "I" messages affect the people in these situations?* —*How did using an "I" message make you feel about yourself?* —*Why do "I" messages tend to lighten up tense situations?*

Resources

Armstrong, Thomas, Ph.D. *In Their Own Way,* Los Angeles: J.P. Tarcher, Inc., 1987.

Ball, Geraldine, Ph.D. *The Magic Circle - Human Development Program, Pre-Kindergarten - Level VI*, San Clemente, California: Magic Circle Publishing, 1974.

Bloomfield, Harold H. *Making Peace With Your Parents*, New York: Random House, 1983.

Borba, Michele. *Esteem Builders*, Rolling Hills Estates, California: Jalmar Press, 1989.

Branden, Nathaniel. *The Psychology of Self Esteem*, New York: Bantam Books, 1971.

Briggs, Dorothy Corkille Briggs. *Your Child's Self-Esteem*, Garden City, NY: Doubleday, 1970.

Brown, George I. *Human Teaching for Human Learning: An Introduction to Confluent Education*, New York: Viking Press, 1971

Buscaglia, Leo. *Love*, Greenwich, CT: Fawcett Books, 1972.

Buscaglia, Leo. *Living, Loving & Learning*, Thorofare, NJ: Charles B. Slack, Inc., 1982.

Chase, Larry. *The Other Side of the Report Card*, Santa Monica, CA: Goodyear Publishing Co., 1975.

Clark, Barbara, Ph.D. *Optimizing Learning*, Columbus, Ohio: Merrill Publishing Co.,1986.

Davis, Robbins, McKay, and Eshelman. *The Relaxation & Stress Reduction Workbook*, Oakland,California: New Harbinger Publications, 1988.

Fanning, Patrick. *Visualization for Change*, Oakland, California: New Harbinger Publications, Inc., 1988.

Fluegelman, Andrew. *The New Games Book*, New York: Doubleday/Dolphin, 1976.

Frey, Diane, Ph.D. and Carlock, Jesse C., Ph.D. *Enhancing Self Esteem*, Muncie, Indiana: Accelerated Development, Inc., 1989.

Gardner, Howard. *Frames of Mind, The Theory of Multiple Intelligences*, New York: Basic Books, Inc., 1983.

Ginott, Haim. *Between Teacher and Child,* New York: MacMillan, 1972.

Glasser, William. *Schools Without Failure*, New York: Harper, 1966.

Gordon, Thomas. *Teacher Effectiveness Training*, New York: Peter H. Hyden, 1974.

Helmstetter, Shad, Ph.D. *What to Say When You Talk to Your Self*, New York: Pocket Books, 1986.

Hendricks, Gay and Wills, Russel. *The Centering Book*, Englewood Cliffs, NJ: Prentice-Hall, 1975

Hendricks, Gay and Roberts, Thomas B. *The Second Centereing Book*, Englewood Cliffs, NJ: Prentice-Hall, 1977.

Herrmann, Ned. *The Creative Brain*, Lake Lure, North Carolina: Brain Books, 1988.

Houston, Jean. *The Possible Human*, Los Angeles: J. P. Tarcher, Inc., 1982.

Jampolsky, Gerald G. *Love is Letting Go of Fear*, Millbrae, CA: Celestial Arts, 1979.

Jampolsky, Gerald G. *Teach Only Love*, New York: Bantam Books, 1983.

Jensen, Eric P. *Super Teaching*, Dubuque, Iowa: Kendall Hunt Publishing Co., 1988.

Leonard, George. *Education and Ecstacy*, New York: Dell, 1968.

Le Page, Andy, Ph.D. *Transforming Education*, Tampa, Florida: Oakmore House Press, 1987.

Maslow, Abraham. *Toward a Psychology of Being*, Princeton: Van Nostrand, 1968.

Moorman, Chick, and Dishon, Dee. *Our Classroom: We Can Learn Together*, Englewood Cliffs, NJ: Prentice Hall, 1977.

Ostrander, Sheila and Schroeder, Lynn. *Superlearning*, New York: Delacorte Press, 1979.

Resources *(Continued)*

Palomares, U. H. and Logan, B. A. *A Curriculum on Conflict Management,* San Clemente, California: Magic Circle Publishing, 1975.

Palomares, Uvaldo, Ed.D. and Ball, Gerry, Ph.D. *Grounds for Growth,* San Clemente, California: Magic Circle Publishing, 1980.

Peck, M. Scott. *The Road Less Traveled,* New York: A Touchstone Book, Simon and Schuster, 1978.

Purkey, William. *Self-Concept and School Achievement,* Englewood Cliffs, NJ: Prentice-Hall, 1970.

Purkey, William and Novak, John. *Inviting School Success* (2nd edition). Bellmont, CA: Wadsworth Publishing Co., 1984.

Reasoner, Robert. Building Self-Esteem: *Teacher's Guide and Classroom Materials* (Elementary Level), 577 College Avenue, Palo Alto, CA 94306: Consulting Psychologists Press, 1982.

Restak, Richard M., M.D. *The Mind,* New York: Bantam Books, 1988.

Rogers, Carl. *On Becoming a Person: A Therapist's View of Psychology,* Boston: Houghton Mifflin Co., 1961.

Rose, Colin. *Accelerated Learning,* New York: Dell Publishing Co., 1985.

Satir, Virginia. *Self-Esteem,* Millbrae, CA: Celestial Arts, 1975.

Simon, Sidney B. *I Am Loveable and Capable,* Niles, IL: Argus, 1976.

Simon, Sidney B. *Vulture: A Modern Allegory of Putting Oneself Down,* Niles, IL: Argus, 1977.

Steiner, Claude. *The Original Warm Fuzzy Tale,* Rolling Hills Estates, CA: Jalmar Press, 1977.

Toward a State of Esteem, The Final Report of the California Task-Force to Promote Self-Esteem, and Personal and Social Responsibility, Sacramento, California: California State Department of Education, 1990.

Resources

Vitale, Barbara Meister. *Unicorns are Real: A Right-Brained Approach to Learning*, Rolling HIlls Estates, Jalmar Press, 1982.

Waitley, Denis. *The Winner's Edge*, New York: Times Books, 1980.

Waitley, Denis. *Seeds of Greatness*, Old Tappan, NJ: Felming H. Revell Company, 1983.

Weinstein, Matt and Goodman, Joel. *PLAYFAIR: Everybody's Guide to Noncompetitive Games*, New York: Doubleday/ Dolphin, 1976.

Wells, Harold C. and Canfield, Jack. *About Me (A self-concept curriculum for grades 3-6)*, Chicago, IL: Encyclopedia Brittannica Educational Corporation.

Wells, Harold C. and Canfield, Jack. *100 Ways to Enhance Self-concept in the Classroom*, Englewood Cliffs, NJ: Prentice-Hall, 1976.

Jalmar Press and Innerchoice Publishing are happy to announce

a collaborative effort under which all Innerchoice titles will now be distributed

only through Jalmar Press.

To request the latest catalog of our joint resources for use by teachers, counselors

and other care-givers to empower children to develop inner-directed living and

learning skills

call us at: (800) 662-9662

or fax us at: (310) 816-3092

or send us a card at: P.O. Box 1185, Torrance, CA 90505

We're eager to serve you and the students you work with.